INNOVATE PRODUCTS FASTER

GRAPHICAL TOOLS FOR *ACCELERATING* PRODUCT DEVELOPMENT

john carter | jeanne bradford

TCGen Press, Menlo Park

Warning and Disclaimer

Every effort has been made to make this book as complete and as accurate as possible, but no warranty of fitness is implied. The information provided is on an "as-is" basis. The authors, contributors, and publisher shall have neither liability nor responsibility to any person or entity with respect to any loss or damages arising from the information contained in the book.

ISBN: 1470002906

ISBN-13: 978-1470002909

"Carter and Bradford have created a practical and essential tool to substantially reduce the time-to-market and dramatically improve ROI. A must read for any company bringing technology products to market."
- Ken Cucarola, CFO Teachscape

"We all dread repeating problems of the past. Carter shows us how to dramatically improve product development with practical, and clearly illustrated tools".
- Bharat Desai, Principal, ShalShiv Associates, Bay Area

"Graphical tools like these allow leaders and teams to see to the heart of a new product program, make good decisions faster, and innovate in more dimensions than possible from staring at numbers on a spreadsheet."
- Scott Elliott, Consultant and former HP Lab Manager

"They say a picture is worth 1000 words, Innovating products faster, is worth 1000 pictures. John Carter does a great job not just explaining his unique product development process, but more importantly giving you the tools to innovate faster yourself. Now you just have to go do it!"
- Jeffrey Harkness, President of Hark Digital, Founder of Diesel Design

"Too often, the critical few tools that innovators really need get mired in the muck of overly verbose academic theory. Carter and Bradford have delivered a book here that cuts right to the chase with a straightforward, practical toolset - ready for use immediately."
- Wayne Mackey, Principal of Product Development Consulting

"Everyone wants to accelerate innovation but Jeanne & John tell you "how" to do it. Their work offers robust tools and guidance to help time-pressed managers create and maintain a lead in innovation – invaluable for anyone concerned with how to create and capture value in rapidly changing environments."
- Dr. Tammy Madsen, Professor of Strategy, Leavey School of Business, Santa Clara University

"Every company wants to innovate products faster. This book will show you how to make it a reality."
- Duncan McNamara, Senior Program Manager, Omnicell, Inc.

"With nearly 35 years of developing challenging, cutting-edge, advanced-technology products, I only wish I would have had this book sooner! You have a way of distilling wisdom gained from life lessons into an easy-to-follow set of tools."
- Ken Reindel, Director of Measurement Technology, National Instruments

DEDICATION

I dedicate this book to those who inspire us to achieve the most we can. Throughout my life, I have had many mentors who have made a huge difference in my direction and achievements. These include Dr. Amar Bose, Sherwin Greenblatt, Tom Froeschle, and Joe Veranth at Bose; Tom Hout at the Boston Consulting Group; Cynthia Ringo at DBL; Tom Jacoby at Tymphany; and Mike Hackworth at Cirrus Logic.

We also dedicate this book to our clients who challenge our thinking and bring us to the ground to turn theory into practice.

Last, but not least, to Dr. Edie Goldberg, my understanding wife and life partner.

- John Carter

Over the course of my career, I have been very fortunate to work with extraordinary leaders. They are remarkable mentors who contributed to my success (and the success of many others) through their knowledge, coaching, and support. For their guidance and generosity, I extend my thanks and gratitude to Kerry O'Rourke, David Turner, Andy Felong, and Dennis Stevenson.

I also dedicate this book to the memory of my mother, Adelaide Hooper. She continues to inspire me every day.

- Jeanne Bradford

ACKNOWLEDGMENTS

We would like to acknowledge and thank the following people who helped us in putting this book together:

Garry Dimapilis: a very effective layout guru who turns work around faster than we can generate it.

Jeffrey Harkness: a digital strategist and designer responsible for setting the design standards for the book (including the book cover).

Ashraf Khamis: a superb editor who worked with us on the many drafts of the book.

Laura Lowell: a great mentor and coach for anyone writing a book in this new world of publishing. She is also the creator and editor of the 42 Rules series.

Fagaras Codrut Sebastian: an illustrator who handled our many diagrams with skill and care.

Besides those involved in graphics and editing, we had several authors who contributed exceptional chapters. We would like to acknowledge the following contributors:

Sheila Mello (of Product Development Consulting, Boston): John's former partner and someone from whom he has learned so much. She authored the Product Radar Chart chapter.

Wayne Mackey (also of Product Development Consulting): an amazing consultant who wrote the Schedule Estimating Matrix chapters. Wayne is a master of all things related to metrics.

Scott Elliott (of TechZecs, San Francisco): contributed the chapter on using Mind Maps to help with risk management. Scott has worked with John for years and is someone we can always rely on for his insight (and great sense of humor).

Barbara Shannon (of TSG The Solutions Group, Oakland): wrote the chapter on Change Communication. Barbara is a master of change management and organizational transformation.

Stan DeMarta (of Pleasanton, California): a versatile manager and consultant with extensive experience in Web 2.0 and embedded software design. Stan contributed to the book's development and is someone we respect for his intellect and drive.

Paul Dandurand (of PIEmatrix, Vermont): provided us with an inspirational view of program management and a way to visualize it. Paul wrote the chapter on Project Portfolio at a Glance.

TABLE OF CONTENTS

EXECUTION

ORGANIZATION

PROCESS

APPENDIX

INTRODUCTION

The prevailing view of innovation is wrong. The traditional view of product development is that there is a fundamental dichotomy between innovation and time-to-market. You can have one or the other, but not both. However, this is not a fundamental law like Newton's law or the second law of thermodynamics, but rather a simplistic view of management that likes to use the excuse "one way or the other" to defend a long-held belief.

Our experience is based on our work with some of the biggest and best technology companies in the world. During the course of our 25+ years in product development, we have observed a pattern that is disturbing and wasteful. Most companies continue to make the same mistakes over and over again in product development. We're talking about big mistakes. We see companies delivering new product programs that are over budget, late to market, and lacking the expected functionality. We often see companies that desperately need to innovate fall short. We don't expect these failures to go away anytime soon, but we can minimize their frequency and impact. The best practices in this book provide managers with tools that will help them make better decisions.

Managers are busy and inundated with large volumes of information, yet they still want to learn about new product development best practices. We wanted to provide these best practices in a print format that is fast and easy to consume. We organized this book for professionals who need instant answers. These professionals are used to getting instant answers on the internet and are not interested at all in wading through a tome to find the answers they need.

There is a lack of contemporary product development best-practice materials that address the new forms of development that have taken root over the last five years. Managers are thirsty for modern tools to address modern problems. In most cases, it is not that managers are reluctant to try new methods; they simply don't know about them.

Companies can have both innovation and speed. It requires mastery of tools and methodologies that will support managers in making better decisions faster. We're not talking about heavy processes or systems that require large IT installations. We're talking about tools that managers can quickly understand and implement. They are tactically straightforward, but strategically powerful. We have tested them in over 50 of our client engagements with measurable successful outcomes. You can apply them across different industries and a wide range of organizations from startups to Fortune 100 companies. To address the need to get useful information in a condensed, straightforward manner, we designed the book into "bite-sized" chapters. You don't need to read the entire book to realize its value. We organized it in a way that allows you to quickly identify the tools you need to solve your biggest problems first.

Innovating Products Faster

There is a constant dialog between those who think that process is evil and destroys any innovation inside an organization, and those who think that process is their savior and can cure all ills. The truth for your organization does not lie in the middle, but off the continuum between these extreme points. Why? Because there are many organizations, including Apple and Google, that are recognized as the most innovative companies in America by Fast Business for having process discipline and encouraging innovation. You can have a highly innovative company and, at the same time, a repeatable development process. Process and innovation can and do coexist. The Product Innovation Process describes an overall methodology that depicts the key milestones in the development process. This process description is above specific engineering methodologies such as waterfall or agile methods.

The beauty of this process is that there are only three checkpoints in your overall product lifecycle. These three checkpoints are defined interactions between the management team and the core cross-functional development team. Rather than being reviews or gates, the check-ins are more like updates between the team and management that allow each party to sync up and ensure alignment on the most important product and project attributes. They are more like peer-to-peer discussions than a critical, hierarchical, and stress-filled review.

Product Innovation Process

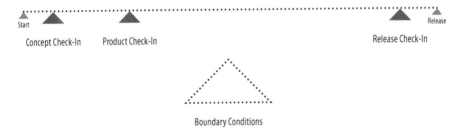

Start   Release

Concept Check-In   Product Check-In   Release Check-In

Boundary Conditions

In the process diagram that shows the methodology, time flows from left to right, and the triangles indicate the key formal interaction points between the team and management. The position of each triangle illustrates the approximate time that a check-in will take place. You specify the boundary conditions at the Concept Check-in and refine them at the Product Check-in. As long as the project stays within the bounds, you do not need any more check-ins until the release. The Release Check-in (near the launch of the project) ensures that the product will meet or exceed expectations because, at this point, all test data is available to management in order to make the launch decision.

Check-ins rather than reviews

There are three defined check-ins and an opportunity to check in if the team believes there is potential for the project to miss its objectives. The first check-in is the **Concept Check-in**, where the management team aligns your project with the current strategic priorities and outlines its major objectives. The second check-in is the **Product Check-in**, where you finalize the definition, describe a rough schedule, and complete a high-level design that demonstrates feasibility. You can often perform this check-in just before the team commits large expenses to the project. The third and final check-in is the **Release Check-in**, which is the point of no return where your organization assesses its capability to launch the product. The areas of focus in this check-in include customer support capability, product quality, and product performance.

The check-in that really makes this process support innovation is one that is triggered when a project exceeds its boundary conditions. **The Out-of-Bounds Check** occurs when the team believes they will not meet the major program goals. Your team has enormous latitude for innovation during the entire product lifecycle, with very little meddling from management and the elimination of time-consuming reviews. By helping your management and team agree on the areas of major emphasis and empowering the core team to manage them, we have set up a situation for success and creativity rather than a stressful environment filled with micromanagement.

Lean process is enabled by trust

Management now places more trust in product development teams. The greater trust allows the team to have ownership and engagement. It fits with the new style of delegation where teams are truly empowered. In addition, so many organizations are struggling with so much process that they are choking on bureaucracy. We are finding that many organizations, especially the more mature ones, are cutting back on process complexity. They follow a path toward a leaner process, but still hold on to some of the tenets of rapid development, including a small number of team-on-team interactions, the core-team concept, and team meetings to assess the cross-functional risks.

This method also promotes rapid communication of a possible problem or project failure. By following the Out-of-Bounds Process, there is a blameless way to react to a "boundary break" and make the best decision for your company, which may include cancelling the project.

Benefits of the Product Innovation Process includes:

- **Encourages innovation** by empowering the team
- **Increases motivation** due to the trust placed in the team
- **Facilitates speed** since the team is empowered to make decisions
- Keeps the team **focused on the core value propositions**
- Is a **repeatable** lightweight process

Growth by innovation

If we look at the key elements that companies now focus on, the one that frequently rises to the top is innovating new products. The opportunity to grow from geographic expansion, deeper domestic distribution, or more SKUs has passed. Sourcing costs have dropped dramatically by going to low-cost regions, so you have little more to gain from further optimizing the supply chain. One of the last and most important areas left for bottom-line growth is product and service innovation. Not only can this area help you grow revenues because it defines new product categories, but it can also allow you to gain more margin due to product differentiation.

The Product Innovation Process provides a lightweight and fast method for getting products out quickly. In addition, because most of the interaction is at the front end, there is a greater probability that the product will meet your users' needs because executives are often closer to the customer compared with most development engineers.

Process alone is not sufficient

This process, however, is not a panacea. It stresses leadership capability from both the CEO's and team's viewpoints. Your management team must not meddle, or they it will defeat the purpose of the process. Conversely, your project manager now has much more authority and needs to use it wisely. The biggest change in this new process, besides having fewer check-ins than older processes, is the Out-of-Bounds Check. The project manager must judge the timing and recommendations of the Out-of-Bounds Check, or the process will not be effective and will most likely turn into a finger-pointing session.

While we talk about the need for skilled project managers, there is a heavy responsibility placed upon the other functional members of your cross-functional team. Each member of the core project team must possess collaborative leadership skills in addition to their domain expertise. With an absence of leadership at the team level, projects will unravel when you identify key gaps.

High-Performance Teams

High-performance teams are not only desirable in achieving innovation and speed – they are essential. However, most companies underestimate or overlook the benefit and opportunity that come from high-performance teams. In our work with world-class technology companies, high-performance teams are, quite frankly, part of their DNA and contribute to their competitive advantage. There are many examples of dysfunctional teams that have heroically pushed products over the finish line, but what many do not acknowledge is the opportunity cost of sub-optimal team performance, both in hard costs (delayed revenue, higher product costs, and higher support costs for low-quality products that reach customers) and soft costs (poor product reviews, lack of innovation, team fatigue, and low morale).

We have identified four steps for creating high-performance teams that you can implement across your organization. If you are ready to incorporate high-performance teams as part of your company's DNA and look forward to seeing a measurable improvement in your ability to quickly innovate and deliver winning products to market, here are the things you should do:

Create well-defined roles and responsibilities for the cross-functional team

Defining team roles and responsibilities seems like a trivial task that is more bureaucratic than useful. But the lack of clarity around cross-functional deliverables and dependencies is a key driver in missed opportunities to reduce cycle time. Especially as companies grow in size and expand geographically, a critical characteristic of high-performance teams is well-defined roles and responsibilities. Having clarity around "who is doing what by when" will free up teams to focus on the work required to innovate and deliver products to market. The chapter "Avoiding Gaps Across Functions" provides a tool for graphically defining key deliverables for the cross-functional teams by development phase. This tool will allow you to clarify what your team will deliver in each phase and will help you anticipate and plan for longer-term deliverables. You may also want to consider creating a Team Wheel for each project (from the chapter "Ensuring Project Teams Are Properly Staffed") to clarify roles at the project level as well.

Implement a core-team model

Implementing a core-team model is the most effective way to optimize a project team's performance and ensure that the broader team (often called the extended team) is functioning efficiently. It is particularly critical when the team is large and geographically dispersed. The core-team model consists of four to six functional leads, typically from project management, product management, engineering, design, manufacturing, and quality assurance. They share the responsibility of delivering the project within the defined objectives, while the ultimate responsibility rests with the project manager. With an emphasis on strong leadership skills, the team can serve as an effective nucleus for driving execution, escalating project issues, and managing cross-functional dependencies. This core team, which meets on a frequent basis, is responsible for communicating to the extended team, which is either geographically isolated or in secondary functions.

Empower the core team with a high level of authority

Many times, executives are hesitant to give teams too much leeway in project decision making, and teams are reluctant to accept the responsibility. In world-class companies, we see a consistent trend of pushing a high level of authority to teams. If you set a culture of team accountability across your organization and empower your team to drive daily decision making in support of the overall objectives of the project, you will see measurable gains in their ability to creatively innovate and shorten cycle time. While there are some circumstances where an autocratic leadership is appropriate, we've found that, if you use it as the norm, it will result over time in lower accountability, de-motivated teams, and delays.

In addition to utilizing a core-team model with well-defined roles and responsibilities, implementing the tools of Product Innovation Process, Boundary Conditions Diagram, and Out-of-Bounds Check will allow you to manage to a framework that defines the boundaries of the team's decision-making authority. Lastly, driving responsibility to the team is a strategic investment in attracting the best talent. High-performance teams consist of high performers – both individually and as a team. High performers thrive on accountability, so, if you push accountability to the team, you will attract the best people in a short period of time.

Create a culture of trust and collaboration

Teams can only achieve high performance if they work in an environment of trust and collaboration. Anything less means that individuals will shift their focus from the common good to their own survival. A true test is examining what happens in your organization when bad things happen. When the schedule is going to slip, a quality issue has stopped the manufacturing line, or the product cost is exceeding the margin target, how does your organization respond? Teams achieve high performance when they know they can deliver bad news (with recommendations for resolution) free of politics and without gaming the data or sugarcoating the message. They achieve high performance because they work in an environment that addresses challenges through collaboration and teamwork. They focus on solving the problem, not finding the guilty and blaming them. And, because you've instilled the authority and trust in them, they do this far faster than those teams that work in an environment of distrust and blame.

High-performance teams will create a competitive advantage. In the end, your ability to rapidly innovate and deliver products to market is in the hands of your people, and the best way we have found to harness the best of people is through high-performance teams.

Strategic Framework

Superior Capabilities in Strategy, Management, and Execution
Supported by Excellence in Organization and Process
Enable You to Innovate Products Faster

In studying some of the world's biggest and best technology companies, we have found that mastering the five core disciplines can lead organizations to both innovation and time-to-market success. The five core disciplines required to innovate products faster are:

- ⚙ **Strategy**: providing the vision and actionable plan in support of corporate/ organizational goals

- ⚙ **Management**: the set of behaviors that support the strategy

- ⚙ **Execution**: operational excellence in hitting timelines and budgets

- ⚙ **Organization**: providing the capability and structure to support strategy, management, and execution

- ⚙ **Process**: methods that describe how the organization should act to support strategy, management, and execution

Most companies demonstrate varying levels of competency in each of these areas. However, in order for companies to enjoy both innovation and time-to-market success, they need to consider the fact that there is a multiplier effect by improving competency at the top of the model first.

Three parts of the framework are contained in the "strategy-to-product cycle", which consists of strategy, management, and execution. It is one of the most important business cycles (probably second to the order-to-cash cycle). An organization that cannot optimize this cycle will never be able to effectively compete. If organizations execute these areas well with an emphasis on (and a supporting culture of) innovation, they will see innovative outcomes. On the other hand, if they just focus on the lower levels of the model (organization and process), they will only see marginal results. The organization and process areas are supporting elements that ensure that the strategy-to-product cycle is as optimal as possible and allow organizations to minimize time-to-market. For example, Amazon, Apple, Google, and Salesforce are companies that have mastered the strategy-to-product conversion process. It is clear that they have a strategy driven by new products, and they execute it well.

The next element in the framework is organization. The success of your product development process fundamentally relies on people. Building a world-class organization is one of the most important roles of management. The companies that succeed in ensuring they have the right resources at the right time to support emerging technologies and core programs will enjoy a competitive advantage in the market. Those that don't will fall behind.

Lastly, we would like to emphasize the importance of process in our framework. Optimizing processes will ensure that you get the most out of the organization and successfully execute the strategy. Without having processes in place to ensure that you gather proper requirements, form the right teams, and have a product free from defects before launch, there is no way you can convert strategy to products. In our work with clients, we frequently see a lack of understanding of how process can support the success of a company delivering to its objectives. Too many times, we see the wrong amount of process applied – either too much, which overburdens teams and slows them down, or too little, which prevents them from scaling and causes them to repeat mistakes. We subscribe to the application of "just right" processes, which allow teams to optimize process implementation to support their business.

How to Use this Book

We wrote this book to help break down this misconception about innovation versus time-to-market. Our goal is to provide managers and their teams with a handbook of best practices that can allow them to achieve both goals simultaneously. The book serves as a graphical summary of the most practical tools that will help teams be more innovative. We organized it around the five core disciplines in the framework and provided a core subset of best practices for each.

We suggest that you look at the appendix before getting started. In the appendix, we recommend a set of solutions based on some of the most common problems. For example, if you are trying to improve predictability, we have suggested a shortlist of the key best practices we find helpful for optimizing predictability. We have also addressed defining products, managing change, minimizing risk, creating effective teams, implementing social media solutions, and many others.

Each chapter consists of a single, stand-alone best practice. We constructed the book in this manner to allow you to choose the tools that are most important to you without the need to consume the entire book before you receive value. We organized each chapter into three sections: (1) a narrative describing the tool and its benefits; (2) a visual representation of the tool; and (3) a case study that applies the tool.

The case studies are of three fictional companies that we use throughout the book to help make the application of the tools richer and more relevant and demonstrate that you can apply these tools across companies of widely varying size and complexity. The companies include a small energy-monitoring company, a medium-sized consumer internet company, and a large networking solutions maker. You can apply almost all of the best practices to hardware, software, cloud, device, or service development.

The 40 best practices come from many sources including ourselves, our clients, fellow consultants, literature, and our academic associates. We offer all these best practices as tools that we have personally implemented. Wherever possible, we provide references where you can discover more information.

Fictional Company Settings

In order to illustrate how the best practices can help your organization, we have created three hypothetical companies to provide the context for the best practices and show how you can apply them and what results you may see. Although the companies and results are fictional, they are representative of very real environments. We have tried to find three companies from a range of settings to demonstrate that the practices are not limited to very large companies, but can apply to a wide variety of situations. The three fictional companies include a clean technology startup (CleanCo), a rapidly growing and profitable consumer internet company (WebCo), and a large and slowly growing networking company (NetCo). Any similarity between these fictional companies and real companies is strictly coincidental.

CleanCo

The clean technology startup provides software as a service (SaaS) that monitors energy usage for businesses to minimize their energy costs. Located in Austin, Texas, the founder-funded company has about 20 employees. They sell their product to large Fortune 500 companies.

They are currently going through their first product launch, and it is critical that they manage their budget and time-to-market. They have limited process management and use rudimentary tools, but they compensate for this by using agile development methods with quick turns and multiple iterations. They are trying to bring in the schedule to hit the next tradeshow, which is four months in the future.

The team consists of the CEO and product visionary, Wendy, the CTO and co-founder, Peter, and the versatile marketing manager, Bill.

WebCo

WebCo is a relatively profitable, agile, and quickly growing Web 2.0 company. This consumer internet company sells a subscription service that allows consumers to manage their finances. They currently have 200 people and have had their third round (C-round) of venture funding. There are large entrenched competitors whom they need to steal market share from in order to succeed.

Currently, they are undergoing a transition from a single product to a multiple product family portfolio. Because they have grown the company without growing the supporting infrastructure, they need scalable processes and new decision-making methods. They also need to be able to share data and reports across the company and manage the growing headcount in three geographically distant places (Silicon Valley, Research Triangle Park, and Vietnam).

The team consists of the newly installed CEO, Rajiv, a professional manager highly focused on execution; the CMO, Ray, who has a long history in consumer internet; Fred, the CTO/VP of engineering and a 25-year veteran of software development; Brian, the project manager; and Molly, the product manager.

NetCo

NetCo is a market share leader in the networking equipment space with over 50,000 employees. The company is located in the Research Triangle Park area. They are in the global telecommunications market, selling to Fortune 100 organizations, the military, and the government. They have grown quickly in the past, but now their growth rate is slowing.

They have a sophisticated development process with many defined management approvals combined with a heavy dose of process to ensure that they can deliver very reliable networking gear. They are currently revamping their product development process, which requires cultural change, project management, and a new technology to support the wiki-based team communication tool. This change will affect over 10,000 engineers. What makes the rollout even more difficult is the globally dispersed and matrix management system already in place.

The team responsible for this new development process consists of the VP of HR, Betty, who (despite her title) is more focused on tactical HR issues than strategic projects. The IT project leader, Chuck, is highly technical and good at handling multiple projects, but lacks people skills. The EVP of engineering, Bill, and the head of the program management office (PMO), Richard, are running the project. Ron, a black belt from the quality organization, is also on the team and provides some deep process experience.

Chapter Timeline

Below is a visual map of the table of contents containing the 40 tools, displaying when you can apply them. This will help you quickly identify the chapters most useful to you given a particular point in development.

Category	Tool	Concept	Design	Development	Test
Strategy	Technology Roadmap	█	█	█	█
	Product Roadmap	█			
	Product Radar Chart	█			
	Platform Derivative Chart	█	█	█	█
	Comprehensive Innovation Map	█	█	█	█
	Comparative Funding Models	█	█	█	
	Outsourcing Map	█	█	█	█
	Social Community Matrix	█	█	█	█
Management	Risk Mind Map	█	█	█	█
	Risk Management Matrix	█	█	█	█
	Predictive Metrics Tree	█	█	█	
	Nine-step Initiative Plan	█	█	█	
	Requirements Management Matrix	█	█	█	█
	PELmatrix Multi-Project Map	█	█	█	█
	Function Phase Matrix	█	█	█	█
	Boundary Conditions Diagram	█	█	█	
	Out of Bounds Check		█	█	█
	Bug Management Matrix				█
Execution	Team PERT Chart	█	█	█	█
	Lite Schedule Estimating Matrix	█	█	█	█
	Precise Schedule Estimating Matrix	█	█	█	█
	Schedule Prediction Accuracy Chart			█	█
	Task Burn-Down Chart			█	█
	Deliverable Hit Rate Chart			█	█
	Project Efficiency Chart	█	█	█	█
	Community Product Requirements Chart	█	█		
Organization	Circle Dot Chart	█	█		
	Project Team Wheel	█			
	Staffing Ratio Matrix	█	█	█	█
	Attitude Influence Diagram	█	█	█	█
	Change Impact Matrix	█	█	█	█
	Social Innovation Readiness Scorecard	█	█	█	█
	Social Innovation Maturity Scorecard	█	█	█	█
Process	Event Timeline Generator	█	█	█	█
	Four-Fields Map	█	█	█	█
	Dot Voting Chart	█	█	█	█
	Project Escalation Map	█	█	█	█
	Root Cause Diagram	█	█	█	█
	Affinity Diagram	█	█	█	█
	Half-Life Diagram	█	█	█	█

The appendix contains recommendations for combining sets of tools to address the most common problems. For example, lack of predictability, poor product definition, undefined roles, and problems with project management.

Strategy

Strategy: Definition

For our purposes, we define strategy as "the art of devising or employing plans toward a goal[1]." Specifically, we are focused on the role product strategy plays in helping the organization achieve its defined objectives. Product strategy is a subset of the corporate strategy, which includes the additional elements of finance, mergers and acquisitions, operations, and sales.

An effective product strategy provides a framework by which you can develop and execute tactical plans to achieve the strategy. Key elements to include in a product strategy are: (1) the product roadmap; (2) the product delivery process; and (3) the operational goals and key metrics for measuring product delivery progress and success. In considering each element, your management team should address both external factors (competition, market, customers, intellectual property, regulation, and geography) and internal factors (competencies, existing product lines, infrastructure, and business model) to ensure the strategy is robust.

The most important output of the strategy process is the creation of the product roadmap, which describes the product portfolio under development over time. It may also show the relationship between product variants and product platforms and how the products may be perceived in the marketplace.

The second element (product delivery process) addresses factors such as the creation of an offshore facility, partnerships, or subcontracts. Your organization's capabilities and physical capacity and/or supply chain objectives determine these factors. Strategic considerations for how to go about product creation and delivery are almost as critical as the definition of the products themselves.

Finally, your strategy should include your operational goals and metrics for product development, such as goals for customer satisfaction or the percentage of revenue from new products. For example, within your portfolio of products, you may direct 10% of the R&D budget toward "new, new" products (those products that involve new technologies and new markets). In this case, the metric you choose should depend on your company's risk profile, which governs the balance between breakthrough and incremental product developments.

Why Is This Section Important in Supporting Innovation and Time-to-market?

The role of strategy in innovation and time-to-market is to define the degree of risk tolerance of your organization and the relative emphasis on speed. You can accomplish your innovation goals by setting your tolerance for risk and then agreeing on the allocation of funding for exploratory ideas. You can communicate this tolerance through the product roadmap in terms of funding targets, such as new generation platforms, derivative products, and incremental products within the larger context of marketing and sales objectives. In most cases, this funding comes at the expense of other lower-risk/lower-revenue projects.

The product strategy also defines the relationship between innovation, time-to-market, and customer satisfaction (quality). All organizations would like to be known as market leaders in all three areas, but, in reality, very few are. However, there are many ways for an organization to be a leader in both time-to-market and innovation (in two of the three areas), and that is what this book is about. There are enduring examples that describe the importance of time-to-market and how it can be a determinant of market share as illustrated in *Competing Against Time* by Stalk and Hout[2]. The strategy should indicate the relative priority between time-to-market and innovation, which can help teams in making tradeoff decisions. This sounds easy, but it is one of the more difficult challenges for management.

Finally, product strategies do not have to be complicated or onerous to develop, but they do need to communicate a vision that will support you in delivering products that provide a differentiated experience in the marketplace. One company we worked with had the following concise product strategy: "We render great visual experience in the smallest package possible."

Use Cases Where You Apply These Tools

This section consists of chapters that illustrate both the "what" and the "how" of strategy. The chapters on roadmaps, radar and derivative charts, and innovation maps show how to derive clear product strategies and create better innovations faster. The following chapters on funding, outsourcing, and social communities illustrate the strategic thinking that goes into the various mechanisms for executing the strategy.

Chapter & Tool Listing

Title	Tool
Anticipating Future Technology Trends	Technology Roadmap
Clarifying Your Product Direction	Product Roadmap
Making Intelligent Product Tradeoffs	Product Radar Chart
Maximizing the Value of Your Platform	Platform Derivative Chart
Creating Better Innovations Faster	Comprehensive Innovation Map
Funding Models for New Business Units	Comparative Funding Models
Harnessing the Global Workforce	Outsourcing Map
Getting the Most out of Social Communities	Social Community Matrix

[1] Merriam-Webster Dictionary, 10th Edition, Merriam-Webster, Incorporated, Springfield, MA. 1996

[2] George Stalk Jr. and Thomas M. Hout, *Competing Against Time*, Free Press, 1990

Anticipating Future Technology Trends
Technology Roadmap

What Is the Tool?

The discussion and critical thinking that go into the creation of a Technology Roadmap can produce more value than the roadmap itself. This tool is fundamentally different from a Product Roadmap, which shows products over time from a customer's perspective. The Technology Roadmap shows technologies over time from a researcher's perspective. One of the organizing principles is that technologies form one stream of activities, product timetables form another stream of activities, and the Technology Roadmap ties these two streams together by indicating which underlying technologies will be mature enough to incorporate in a given product release.

In a horizontal bar-chart format, your technologies are indicated by groups of elements that you can link together logically in terms of the major architectural blocks that describe the key technologies at the highest levels. For example, for a laptop computer, the groups could include CPU, display, storage, power management, and mechanical components. You can then break down the underlying technology components in each group and represent their lifetimes as a bar over time, with the estimated delivery date as the most important element displayed.

In order to produce a robust Technology Roadmap, you need to invest time to determine the key technologies that will go into your product now and many years into the future. Your suppliers and partners are often a good source of key technology input to your roadmap, but you have to be the judge of the degree of realism placed into their schedules.

Time spent out of the office developing technology partners is a critical part of a technology manager's job. As more and more competitive advantage comes from outside the company, you cannot underestimate the importance of scouting for new technologies. By combining and comparing external technologies with internal capabilities, you will clarify your internal research (or advanced development) initiatives.

The second portion of the Technology Roadmap is the product timeline, which is a horizontal bar chart that shows the launch target for each product at a monthly or quarterly granularity. It shows your products as grouped families, much like how you bundle the technology elements together in groups. The beauty of the Technology Roadmap is that it allows for a larger perspective of the technologies that you can anticipate for a given product timetable by looking at a vertical line drawn down from the product through the technologies below. It is a living document that you should update frequently (typically quarterly) as the technologies and product shift over time.

Visualization

The visualization chart below shows the technology elements that go into a consumer electronics product (as shown in the first column). Two internal paths (develop and research) and one external path (supplier) delineate the various technology elements. The chart shows the importance of these technology elements on the right-hand side along with an estimate of their competitive position.

Technology Roadmap

Technology Element	2005	2006	2007	Importance Low	Importance Med	Importance High	Competitive Position Low	Competitive Position Med	Competitive Position High
Amplifiers									
						CF		C	F
					C	F		C	F
					C	F	C	F	
Drivers									
						CF			CF
						CF			CF
					CF			CF	
						CF		C	F
						CF		C	F
						CF		CF	
					C	F	C		F
Signal Processing									
						CF	C		F
						CF	C	F	
						CF		CF	
						CF	C	F	
					CF		C		F
Wireless									
						CF	C	F	
					C	F	C	F	
				C	F		C	F	
					C	F	CF		
Human Factors									
					C	F	C	F	
						CF	C		F

Legend: Technology Source — Develop · Supplier · Research

Legend: Status C = Current F = Future (2-3 Years)

What's New?

The most important trend that confronts your technology managers is that partners now provide a greater portion of a given product than ever before – semiconductor suppliers, overseas manufacturers, and internet APIs (application programming interfaces). The earliest example of this trend was the realization that the brand of a personal computer maker did not matter as much as the key suppliers. For example, Intel and Microsoft determine much more of the capabilities of a personal computer than do PC manufacturers such as HP or Dell[1].

Benefits

- **Highlights the key deficiencies** in your products that you need address
- Allows you to **determine the specific technologies** that you can incorporate in a given product
- Helps you **anticipate risks** by allowing you a degree of visibility into the future
- **Illustrates potential areas of exposure** and, conversely, the areas of untapped competitive advantage that you can pursue
- **Improves cooperation and teamwork** by linking management, engineering, and marketing together

Which Business Problems Does the Tool Solve?

A technology strategy, as embodied in a Technology Roadmap, has a critical role in ensuring that you stay ahead of the competition. All businesses, even service businesses, can obtain competitive advantage by having a well-defined technology strategy that supports customer delight. Not only does this process help you keep ahead of the competition, it also prevents you from being caught by the delay of a new component because you have set up a monitoring system that is ready with alternatives.

What Else Should You Know?

Creating a dynamic Technology Roadmap is not for the faint of heart. The biggest factors to consider before engaging in this process are its difficulty and time requirements. Not only does it require a significant amount of focused time, it also requires a deep understanding of what distinguishes you from your competitors and, most importantly, an understanding of what customers value. This is not a one-time event. You need to update the map on a regular basis and review it with management every quarter.

This map is of no value if you do not communicate it to management. The real benefit of a Technology Roadmap is to influence corporate strategy. One of the best ways to do this is to consider the Technology Roadmap an important input to the yearly strategy process.

Case Study

WebCo, a 200-person startup, is transitioning from being a single-product company to having multiple product lines. One of the new product families of their software subscription services includes operation with tablet computers. This new product family is now reliant on partners more than ever, so it is important to understand the technology evolution of the partners and the underlying tablet technologies. In order to ensure the new product family is a market share winner, Ray, the chief marketing officer is counting on Fred's team to deliver some new technologies. Fred, the head of engineering, has decided to put together a Product Technology Roadmap showing the product family and the supporting core technologies to show Ray specifically how his products will be built.

After visiting several Original Design Manufacturers (ODM), participating in open-source conferences, and attending the IFA consumer electronics show, Fred has been able to come up with an updated Technology Roadmap and fleshed out key risk items including a backup partner for multi-touch technology.

---

[1] Andrew S. Rappaport and Shmuel Halevi, "The Computerless Computer Company," Harvard Business Review, 1991, http://hbr.org/1991/07/the-computerless-computer-company/ar/1, accessed September 2011

Clarifying Your Product Direction
Product Roadmap

What Is the Tool?

Product Roadmaps often serve two masters and fail both. On one hand, the sales team uses them to close a sale as they insert the customer's key wish into the product plan. On the other hand, product management uses them to assure the CEO that they plan to support their vision even though engineering has not looked at those roadmaps.

These two use cases totally miss the point of the power of a well-executed Product Roadmap. The Product Roadmap is best described as a visual explanation of a company's strategy. As a result, it helps align engineering, marketing, sales, support, and the C-suite toward common product development goals. Besides being a visual tool to communicate strategy, a Product Roadmap can inspire innovation because it signals the key areas that are the strongest differentiators. It can also inspire execution in that it helps to communicate platform and derivative strategies and illustrates how these unfold over time.

A Product Roadmap is a graphical representation of a set of related products over time (typically two product cycles or 24-36 months) with, at most, a monthly granularity (but often shown with quarterly resolution). The vertical axis is strategically the most important, as it displays the products, how they relate to each other, and how they might relate to the competition in ways that matter. Although one of the most common vertical axes is cost, it can also be speed or the key-feature parameter.

Visualization

The Product Roadmap shows the evolution of product features and price points over time. The vertical axis is often cost, and the horizontal axis is time. This diagram reveals the timing and relationship of a consumer and professional software offering.

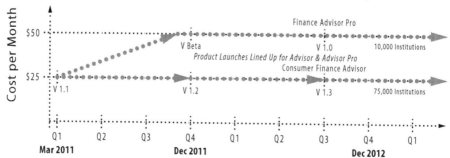

WebCo's Finance Advisor Product Roadmap

What's New?

Articulating a common vision for success is hardly a new concept, but it is rarely accomplished in a manner that ensures that all stakeholders and contributors truly understand the vision. What is new is the importance of how product differentiation supports your competitive advantage. When product innovation is more important than distribution strategy or financial engineering, the Product Roadmap becomes the most important planning document for any company that aspires to be number one or two in their market.

Your company can often generate a product plan from a variety of sources that have functionally focused views on what problems you are trying to solve. However, your views are not always useful because they do not incorporate sufficient inputs to be reliable or comprehensive. A robust Product Roadmap is a cross-functionally created document that the C-suite reviews and approves. You should not communicate it outside the company, but rather use it to focus the company on the sequence of products developed over time.

This is a living document that serves as a repository for those project ideas that you can place into the product development process. You should review and update it on a quarterly basis at a minimum.

Benefits

- Provides a clear visual **representation of product strategy**
- **Inspires the organization to think about supporting innovations** to drive parameters of importance
- **Inspires the organization to see how they might get operational leverage** by creating derivative products off of platforms
- **Sets expectations** for when the organization will deliver products/services to market
- **Serves as an organizing principle** for decisions around technology requirements, resource allocation, and product positioning

Which Business Problems Does the Tool Solve?

Often individuals and managers in organizations say that there is no strategy, or, if it exists, they say it is poorly communicated. An often-referenced Product Roadmap allows for better strategic alignment and, as a result, greater engagement. It also helps the executive management and product marketing teams manage the inputs to the new product development process. While a Product Roadmap should never preclude competitive reactions or innovation from "cutting in front of the line", it does provide an active plan for what should be next on deck for development. The working use of a Product Roadmap actively helps innovation in at least two dimensions. First, it communicates through the vertical axis what is important to the organization. Second, it provides a strategic context for engineers, researchers, and other creative individuals to come up with concepts that support, complement, and extend the strategic intent of the roadmap.

Finally, in the world of global product development, Product Roadmaps can communicate the international launch strategy so that the organization plans the timing for entry into different markets and anticipates regulatory approvals, language, localization, and standards.

What Else Should You Know?

In order to be most useful, the Product Roadmap must anticipate and lead changes in the market, in the channels, in the supply, and in the competitive landscape. So "shooting in front of the duck" is important because, in most industries, you have to anticipate what your competitors will have in the market when you come out with your product 12 months from now. Often Product Roadmaps are useless because the focus is on some banal graphics of bubbles on an arrow. A meaningful Product Roadmap should be a two-axis graph showing with detail and accuracy the timetable for launches, the relationships between products, and the delineated features that show how one product differs from the other.

Case Study

WebCo, which delivers leading financial management software as a service, is experiencing great acceptance of their initial product launch and is now focused on multiple offerings of the product for a differentiated performance/value market. They are constructing a strategy to divide the product offering to compete between a high-performance/high-feature offering and an entry-level product. To ensure that the market does not consider them a one-product company, they want to construct a Product Roadmap to communicate their vision for the success of their offerings. They also aim to ensure that the teams and technology are in place to deliver a successful portfolio of products over the next five years.

They are branching from their roots as a direct-to-consumer company to add a high-margin product line that would be oriented toward financial planners. Their unique selling proposition (USP) is ease of use and simplicity of operation, which they need to have for both markets. Their other USP is connectedness with other financial institutions so that their customers can get their statements electronically and track their income and expenses. Their primary problem is how to leverage as much of the core platform as possible and still provide additional features for the financial planners. The company plans to go through a product planning and product road-mapping activity. The executives have started by reviewing the USPs of the two products. They have all agreed that the USPs are the selling price, user experience, and number of financial institutions. Ray (the CMO), Fred (the CTO), and Rajiv (the CEO) own, support, and approve this process respectively. In order to speed up the market analysis and the creation of the chart itself, Ray has borrowed Molly, a project manager who has really good research skills and can help with competitive evaluation and document creation.

The outcome of this six-week process is that the executive team has created and agreed on a Product Roadmap. One of the benefits of this process is that they have clearly defined the USPs as the number of financial institutions they can exchange data with, the monthly subscription cost, and the simplicity of the user interface (maintained for the more complex product sold to financial planners and measured as the average time to do three tasks on the website). The second benefit is that everybody involved in supporting the roadmap has done resource planning at a high level.

Making Intelligent Product Tradeoffs
Product Radar Chart
Sheila Mello

What Is the Tool?

One of the most basic realities of product development is that limited resources (time, money, or staff) force tradeoffs both at the level of the product portfolio and within individual products. Lacking a methodology for evaluating potential products, companies often make decisions based on unsubstantiated factors such as convenience, the enthusiasm of the lead engineer, or the rank of the executive who cheers the loudest.

The Product Radar Chart offers a way to evaluate and communicate the myriad factors that go into product and portfolio decisions by graphing the key dimensions of a product or concept versus alternatives. Typically, you can use the chart at the Concept Check-in stage when the development team is evaluating alternative concepts or presenting alternative products to management for approval to proceed. You rank each alternative on a scale of one to ten, with the center of the chart representing a value of zero and the outer edge of the spokes representing a value of ten.

Value to the customer is always the most important parameter. Strategic value (how closely a product maps to the company's strategy) and investment intensity (the level of resources required to develop and market the product) also figure heavily into the equation, but they are by no means the only factors. Each factor has a different weight that is used to provide a total summary score. The 10 factors that we show here are those we have found to differentiate winning, strategically-aligned products from those that fail to meet business objectives. This is not, however, a fixed list across all businesses. Each organization needs to ascertain which factors are relevant to its business success.

Using the Product Radar Chart for individual product assessments and comparing the feasibility of competing product ideas can bring transparency and consensus to a process often marked by unclear reasoning and turf battles.

Visualization

The Product Radar Chart shows a comparison of three alternatives. In this case there are eight dimensions of product performance, rated from 0 (minimum achievement) to 10 (maximum achievement). Product 1 has the highest average score, and should be chosen if core competency gaps can be resolved.

Product Radar Chart for Three Potential Products

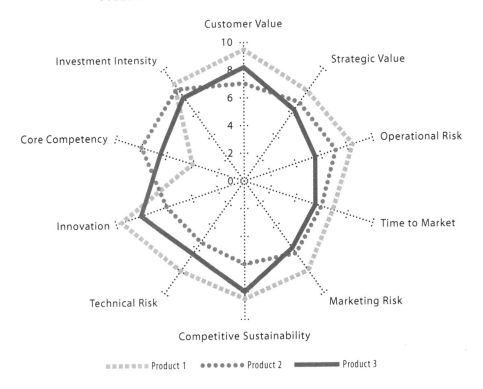

Customer Value
Strategic Value
Investment Intensity
Operational Risk
Core Competency
Time to Market
Innovation
Marketing Risk
Technical Risk
Competitive Sustainability

Product 1   Product 2   Product 3

What's New?

As a product creator, you may have come upon a situation where you needed to choose between product alternatives. This tool addresses the need for differentiation and the creation of a total product that meets visible and invisible needs. One of the newer sets of concepts for creating product alternatives is the so-called "Innovation Tournaments" that Terwiesch and Ulrich[1] first described. Innovation Tournaments and related internet social communities often generate several product concepts at the same time. They often compete for the same resources, so picking the best choice is an essential step. The Product Radar Chart presents a rapid, graphical, and fresh approach for evaluating alternative product concepts.

Benefits

Using a Product Radar Chart lets you organize and communicate information about data feeds related to such disparate aspects of your business as investment intensity, strategic value, customer value, core competencies, innovation, and marketing risk. Once you have this information in visual form, you can:

- **Quickly identify mismatches** between your current strategy and current capabilities.

- **Make informed decisions** about which products to invest in based on how well they map to strategy and to what customers value.

- **Compare** how **different products** fulfill other requirements (such as lowering risk by aligning with core competencies).

- **Make tradeoffs** among various products and among features of individual products.

- **Communicate** tradeoff **decisions** to corporate managers.

Which Business Problems Does the Tool Solve?

Companies usually generate far more ideas than they can afford to pursue. At the corporate level, the question then becomes how to decide which of the many potential products should receive funding. These choices have far-reaching consequences both for the immediate bottom line (will they be successful?) and for the corporate identity. The products a company chooses to develop ultimately determine what kind of company it becomes.

The same tradeoff questions arise at the individual product or project level after you have researched customer needs, generated requirements, and brainstormed potential solutions. How do you decide which among the products' many potential capabilities are worth developing for the final production version?

The Product Radar Chart lets you visually represent a multitude of attributes for portfolio and product decision making in a way that is richer and more versatile than the bubble charts typically used for such evaluations. This makes it an ideal tool for communicating and facilitating discussions of the inevitable trade-offs in managing a product portfolio.

What Else Should You Know?

A beautiful visual representation is worth nothing if you base it on faulty data. Using the Product Radar Chart assumes several prerequisites:

- Your business strategies are clear.
- You have a way to determine customer value.
- You have a process in place to evaluate factors such as operational and technical risk.

At the very highest level, before putting the Radar Chart to use, you need to understand the business your company is in. This represents the very first layer of constraint.

Because the Radar Chart places "customer value" as the central driver of all the other aspects of the business, using the chart assumes that you have a method in place to assess customer value. Ideally, this is a robust, fact-based process that relies on collecting and analyzing data without preconceptions about what customers want.

Another key to using the Radar Chart is to come up with a list of constraints particular to your business or product that will become the spokes of the chart. These might include common constraints such as competitive sustainability, technical risk, and innovation, or more particular ones such as the degree of control your organization can maintain during implementation (for example, the ink-cartridge division of a printer company might make cartridge improvements that rely on the manufacturing decisions that the company's hardware division makes, which limits the direct control the ink-cartridge division can exercise).

Finally, it's important to note that you can use the Radar Chart not only for new-to-the-world products, but also for incremental extensions to existing products and even for non-product improvements, such as customer service or support.

Case Study

Let's look at the case of a company that currently leads the market with its networking products – NetCo. In an effort to remain competitive into the future, the company is looking to expand into adjacent markets with a new product. The EVP of engineering, Bill, and his marketing counterpart will lead this project to discover the "next big thing."

Bill has created a cross-functional innovation team that includes representatives from R&D, support, marketing, and operations, and asked them to recommend a new product based on customer research. Their research and brainstorming process has led to the definition of three potential high-speed routing products (named 1, 2, and 3), each of which scores differently in relation to the company's major constraints.

The team plots the three products on a single Radar Chart (above), with the center of the chart representing a value of zero and the outer edge of the spokes representing higher values. When it comes to the visual representation of your assessment, higher numbers always correspond to more desirable states. This means you may need to reverse rankings depending on whether more or less of a particular attribute is desirable. For example, although a lower operational risk value is better than a higher one, you would assign the lowest operational risk a value of "10" to ensure that it falls at the outside of the spokes. Thus, a quick glance at the Radar Chart would show areas of potential concern for each product.

The Radar Chart above shows that Product 1 outscores Products 2 and 3 in the desirable traits of customer value and innovation. At the same time, however, it has a low value for core competency mapping, meaning that the company may have to outsource product development or invest heavily to bring in the necessary technical expertise. Product 2 takes advantage of existing core competencies, but does not score high on customer or strategic value.

By mapping the three product options on the Radar Chart, the team is able to visualize the relative merits of each option in order to pick the right one.

[1] Christian Terwiesch and Karl Ulrich, *Innovation Tournaments: Creating and Selecting Exceptional Opportunities*, Harvard Business School Press, May 2009

Maximizing the Value of Your Platform
Platform Derivative Chart

What Is the Tool?

Let's start by asking "What is a platform?" According to David Robertson[1], a platform is "the collection of assets that are shared by a set of products." These assets can be divided into four categories:

- Components: the part designs of a product, the fixtures and tools needed to make them, the circuit designs, and the programs burned into programmable chips or stored on disks.

- Processes: the equipment used to make components or to assemble components into products, and the design of the associated production process and supply chain.

- Knowledge: design know-how, technology applications and limitations, production techniques, mathematical models, and testing methods.

- People and relationships: teams, relationships among team members, relationships between the team and the larger organization, and relations with a network of suppliers."

In our discussion, we will recognize the total definition of platform as indicated by the four points above, but our primary focus will be the notion that a platform is "a collection of assets (components) that are shared by a set of products." A Platform Derivative Chart is a diagram that depicts a set of related products over time. This is the most powerful type of Product Roadmap where the relationships between derivatives are highlighted. You may find it the most useful type of roadmap because the horizontal and vertical axes are labeled, the products are precisely mapped, and the positioning is clearly described.

The Platform Derivative Chart is similar to the Product Roadmap, but different in several important ways. We recommend that your organization use both. The Platform Derivative Chart is a technology/design-driven diagram of related products with some underlying common design components. The Product Roadmap shows the portfolio of products under development which may or may not have common technologies. This diagram shows the lifecycle of the platform and the family of derivatives indicating the relationships between the various derivatives. These relationships can be cost, performance, quality, or feature density. For example, in the computer business, the Platform Derivative Chart might show a 15" laptop family where the product platform is the base product and the variants appear at various price points with different feature sets, such as amount of memory, hard disk size, CPU speed, and graphics capability. It is possible for a laptop division to integrate all products on one chart showing where the different platforms exist in the family, again versus price points and feature sets. In addition, it is possible to show competitors on the chart to communicate the relative performance of the product against its competitors.

Your head of product management often creates this chart, and your head of the business unit reviews and approves it. There should be a clear line of sight between the business unit's strategic plan, the Platform Derivative Chart, and the product pipeline. Your internal "customers" of the chart can include engineering, sales, operations, customer service, and related functions. In many organizations, this is the tangible conversion of strategy into product.

Visualization

The chart below shows product plans over the next several years in half-year increments. The vertical axis shows the retail price in subscription costs per month. The dark boxes show the platform development efforts, with the creation of a new platform based on AJAX and HTML5. The chart shows the company has derived a second platform, based on small business needs, from the first, and added balance-sheet capabilities that incorporate depreciation and amortization. The labeling of each derivative shows the key features, such as the lowest-cost version available for mobile devices for only $5 per month.

Platform Derivative Chart

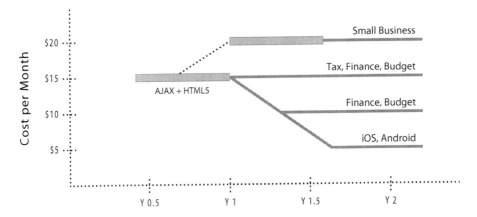

What's New?

Product road mapping has been around for a long time, but there is a new emphasis on the Platform Derivative Chart because many organizations are using ODM/JDM (original design manufacturing/joint design manufacturing) development models where the supplier communicates its roadmap to potential customers. We are also seeing the proliferation of web-based platforms where organizations build products similar in size to those of some very significant companies. One of the best examples is the set of APIs (application programming interfaces) that Facebook has created. Other companies, such as Zynga, are using them to develop very sophisticated games that take advantage of the social networking platform created by Facebook.

Platform thinking also leverages innovation by trying to create the maximum footprint of a given invention as it is commercialized. When you create and productize an invention, you would like to take as much advantage of the invention as possible. Innovation is very precious, and you should try to leverage its application and pay back the investment in the best way possible.

Benefits

- **Maximizes the financial impact** of innovation by spreading over derivative products.
- **Reduces average time-to-market** because it maximizes reuse.
- **Builds alignment in the organization** by focusing development on a few, very valuable design foundations.
- **Reduces development costs** by leveraging the platform.

Which Business Problems Does the Tool Solve?

Platform thinking and the Platform Derivative Chart represent a way of looking at maximizing innovation. More often than not, the platform is the result of many years of research and development and codifies all the efforts resulting from one or more innovative concepts. The platform's greatest benefit is that it maximizes the revenue and business impact of an invention.

Besides having tremendous benefits to sales and profit, the Platform Derivative Chart has internal benefits too, such as reducing engineering expenses and increasing speed and agility. When you leverage the significant design work embodied in a platform, your subsequent product variants will require much less engineering time and less calendar time to bring to market and your new product process will be much more efficient.

What Else Should You Know?

Creating a coherent platform strategy is not easy. The first challenge is that you need an innovation significant enough that you can use it to spawn a family of products. Often organizations create an advanced development group to create the next generation of platforms. They often use social communities for the ideation and creation of next-generation platforms by using the wisdom of the crowd inside and outside the organization. The second challenge is coming up with a system engineering strategy that allows the platform to create derivatives easily. This is a challenge for your principal engineer or product architect to create the total product from an innovative technology. This total product must be easy to modify, so there must be a set of defined interfaces where you can easily add or change different supporting components.

Finally, you need to be patient. Although creating derivative products is routine after you build the platform, the time to come up with a creative platform is highly variable. Platform development is more like research than development, so the timeframes are more unpredictable and the risks are higher compared to normal development efforts. We recommend you use the winning strategy of setting aside an allocation of 10% of the product development budget for new platform creation and not put the platform project in the formal development process until you eliminate the significant risks.

Case Study

WebCo is a relatively profitable and quickly growing Web 2.0 company that has the attributes of agility and growth. This consumer internet company sells a subscription service that allows consumers to manage their finances. They currently have 200 people and have had their third-round (C-round) venture funding.

Currently, they are undergoing a transition from a single product to a multiple product family approach and are migrating to a comprehensive Product Roadmap. The team that will come up with the new platform strategy consists of the newly installed CEO, Rajiv, a professional manager highly focused on execution; the CMO, Ray, who has a long history in consumer internet; and Fred, the CTO/VP of engineering and a 25-year veteran of software development.

Rajiv has challenged Ray to revise and clarify their product strategy and to leverage some promising new technologies coming out of development. Ray has decided to work with Fred to come up with a platform plan and create a Platform Derivative Chart to communicate their thinking to Rajiv and the rest of the organization. Just the two of them, working over two and a half weeks, have come up with a platform concept and a series of derivatives that, if executed correctly, could result in revenues on par with some of the current market share leaders in two to three years. They have done some competitive analysis of two of their biggest competitors in online financial management to see how the innovations in the platform might allow them to capture some of the underserved segments of the market.

Rajiv has approved the resulting plan, as codified in the Platform Derivative Chart, and rolled it out to the organization. As a result of the new platform plan, Rajiv has supplemented the small group working on these new developments with seven additional team members and doubled their budget in order to speed up development.

---

[1] David Robertson, *Platform Product Development*, Baan Company, March 1998

Creating Better Innovations Faster
Comprehensive Innovation Map

What Is the Tool?

There are many different ways for individuals and companies to innovate. Some have been developed through trial and error and others through legend and tribal knowledge. Recently, there have been some significant breakthroughs in how you can manage innovation to achieve better results. For example, group brainstorming, even with a good facilitator, fails to deliver as much as individual creative processes[1].

We have found that companies may benefit from a process we call "Comprehensive Innovation" because it describes a research-verified, end-to-end set of steps that yield the best and most creative ideas. You can apply this three-step method to small problems in as little as a day, or scale it to solve the largest challenges that might span several weeks or more. The steps are Framing, Ideation, and Selection. In each of the three steps, we destroy myths and inject best practices to deliver a process that, if followed, can deliver better results than those of other brainstorming methods.

The first step is to frame the problem. It is said that if Einstein had 20 days to solve a problem, he would like to spend 19 days on defining the problem and leave one day to solve it. A book by McKinsey researchers called *Brainsteering*[2] suggests there are five areas you can use to generate the best, most specific questions:

1. Identifying unsolved customer problems

2. "De-averaging" users and activities

3. Exploring unexpected successes

4. Imagining perfection

5. Discovering unrecognized "headroom" (rules to reexamine or new technologies)

Once you define the questions, it is very important to select the best people to address them. When thinking about your team, it is important to select the right people for the problem at hand, largely ignoring management hierarchy. You can address the organizational politics in the third step.

The second step is to come up with the ideas themselves – Ideation. Here again, research by Terwiesch and Ulrich[3] has indicated that the tried and true group brainstorming method is flawed. Allowing time for individual contemplation ahead of the group process can generate significantly better ideas than those from brainstorming. When running a brainstorming session in the past, you probably found that some people dominated the discussion, not allowing others to contribute their thoughts. You have probably experienced "groupthink" at some point, where one idea that seems to resonate with a vocal minority gets repeatedly reinforced and, therefore, limits the true expansion of the concept. By having an initial individual-thinking session (which takes as little as ten minutes), you can have a significantly improved process because the ideas going into the group session will be stronger and more diverse. Here you can use a group process to come up with ways to improve, modify, or combine ideas in order to get a better concept.

The third step is Selection where you choose ideas and make plans for implementation. There are many alternative modes of selection that you can successfully deploy. The first is the Product Radar Chart that we previously outlined in the book. You should specify the key evaluation dimensions of the chart during the Framing step and then apply them at this final step. Other selection methods are available from ideation software vendors such as Brightidea and Spigit, each of which has unique methods to "graduate" and select ideas. There is also a software tool associated with Innovation Tournaments that you can use, called the Darwinator[3].

After you complete these three steps, you must fund or plan to implement the selected idea. This is crucial for several reasons, including the obvious fact that the idea will not turn into an innovation unless you implement it. The other most important reason is credibility. These group sessions will die out or lack creative energy if the participants notice that you do not act upon the winning ideas. There are two ways that you may consider funding. The first, and most likely, is to insert the idea into the product development process in a fashion so that the idea is "fast tracked" because you have already demonstrated its merit. The second way is to create a skunk-works project where you allow an isolated team to develop the concept by themselves. However, this only postpones the integration of the idea into corporate processes, which must happen at some point to make a commercial success. Finally, you can hide or rename the idea to prevent corporate antibodies from attacking it. UNIX was developed this way, having been described to management as a word processing program for patent applications[4].

Visualization

The chart below shows the Comprehensive Innovation Map, with each box containing two supporting elements. The vertical axis is the degree of abstraction, and the horizontal axis is the time scale (typically one day, but can be up to several weeks). The quality estimate shown in parentheses indicates the relative quality level from 1-5 that each step was performed. Quality scores below 3.0, such as the Ideation step, should indicate that the step should be modified and improved.

Comprehensive Innovation Map

Abstract

Ask the correct questions
Have the appropriate people

Individual ideation time
Building and combining

Evaluation with criteria
Implementation plans & budget

Concrete

Framing	Ideation	Selection	Time
Quality (4.5)	Quality (2.5)	Quality (4.5)	

What's New?

We have been taught to believe that group brainstorming, teamwork, and collaboration can lead to innovation. However, recent research has indicated that group processes don't produce the best ideas[5]. The best innovation outcomes come from a combination of individual creation and group implementation.

Benefits

- ◎ **Ensures strategic alignment** of solutions with real problems
- ◎ Helps you **address simple as well as complex problems**
- ◎ Is **resource efficient** because it is focused, managed, and time-bound
- ◎ Ultimately **improves profit** because it allows you to select and implement good ideas quickly

Which Business Problems Does the Tool Solve?

The Comprehensive Innovation Map allows companies to innovate and generate better ideas faster. Because this method emphasizes both individual thinking and group brainstorming, it also significantly improves team morale.

What Else Should You Know?

Rarely does a technique like this create new breakthrough business areas. Other techniques such as bottom-up, customer-driven, and focused innovations by dedicated researchers most often come up with the biggest breakthroughs. However, for many problems (small and medium sized), the Comprehensive Innovation Map is extremely effective. Its success, however, depends on top management support. In order to get the funding, management at the budgetary level must support the process and its outcomes.

Its success also rests on the quality of the people handling the process. The quality of the people providing the insights and the quality of the facilitator leading the process are two very important ingredients for yielding successful outcomes.

Case Study

CleanCo has run up against a very difficult situation that could bring an end to the company if they do not resolve it. The engineering team has just discovered that they cannot consistently access the utility APIs that allow them to monitor the real-time energy use of major facilities. They have been butting their heads against the problem for two weeks and, finally, Wendy (the CEO) and Peter (the CTO) have agreed to apply this process to this critical problem. Peter has facilitated the process and selected Bill (the marketing manager) and a handful of engineers to help solve the problem. They have hosted an innovation day to go after this problem and created the following agenda to support the process:

Time		Activity
9:00	10:00	Definition of the problem Definition of the radar criteria for selecting a solution
10:00	11:00	Individual problem-solving (at their desks)
11:00	12:00	Group discussion
12:00	1:00	Lunch
1:00	2:00	Initial ranking of top ideas
2:00	3:00	Combining/improving
3:00	4:00	Writing up to five of the best ideas on a poster board (one flip chart)
4:00	5:00	Presentation of ideas to the evaluation team (CEO/CTO/CMO) Next steps on the top two ideas

Before conducting the session, Peter has looked at the Comprehensive Innovation Map and scored each element on a scale from one to five. One means insufficient, three is just sufficient, and five exceeds requirements. The goal of this scorecard is to identify problems before they happen. Any sum below three should be an indicator that something may be wrong. Here are the scores he has assigned:

Framing	
Ask the correct questions	4
Have the appropriate people	5
Average	**4.5**
Ideation	
Individual ideation time	3
Building and combining	2
Average	**2.5**
Selection	
Evaluation with criteria	4
Implementation plans & budget	5
Average	**4.5**

After rating these elements, Peter has decided to expand the agenda and add a half-day session two days later to see how he might build up/enhance the highest-ranking ideas. Although he felt that he needed a day to cover the topics, he settled for half a day because he did not want to burn out the team. After the half-day session, the team has come up with some exceptional ideas. This has left Wendy very confident that they will solve this technical problem.

[1] Karan Girotra, Christian Terwiesch, and Karl T. Ulrich, *Idea Generation and the Quality of the Best Idea*, Management Science, MS-01219-2007.R1, ScholarOne Manuscript Central, 2007

[2] Kevin P. Coyne and Shawn T. Coyne, *Brainsteering*, HarperCollins, 2011

[3] Christian Terwiesch and Karl T. Ulrich, *Innovation Tournaments*, Harvard Business School Press, 2009

[4] Warren Toomey, *The Strange Birth and Long Life of Unix*, IEEE Spectrum, December 2011, p. 34-55

[5] Susan Cain, *The Rise of the New Groupthink*, New York Times, Opinion Section, January 13, 2012.

Models for New Business Units
Comparative Funding Models

What Is the Tool?

You can use this visualization tool to fund innovation programs. Business units that have R&D budgets below that of the corporate average are called "sources." They source revenue allocations to other business units called "sinks" because the R&D budget allocation their sales generate, using the corporate average percentage, is lower than their spending. The sum of the sources and sinks yields the overall average.

This tool helps shift your debate about funding new innovation areas from the political to the strategic. By looking at your funding levels over time, it is possible to communicate to those business unit managers how the budget represents a tradeoff and how they will make strategic allocations in the future based on models not politics.

Visualization

The bar chart shows relative R&D funding as a percentage of sales for three business units. The percentage is the vertical axis, and the years are shown on the horizontal axis. During years 1, 2, and 3 the startup division is funded by reallocating funding from two other units. However, note that R&D spending remains constant at 10% of sales.

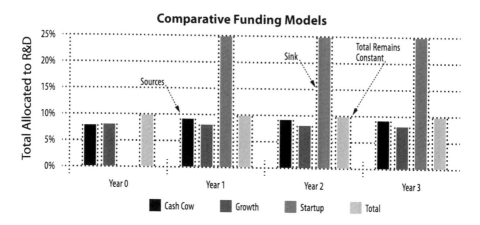

What's New?

Most businesses today are looking to take advantage of innovation or geographic expansion to drive revenue growth, but they lack methods to fund the necessary programs to support expansion. This visualization tool allows your managers the ability to see into the future and justify investments in new areas. It also allows management to communicate this information to shareholders and internal organizations.

Benefits

- **Translation of strategy** into a financial model
- Communicates this model to impacted organizations to **reduce politics and enable support of the vision**
- It can help create a more **efficient budgeting process**
- **It allows you the ability to forecast** the time at which business units turn from consumers of product development allocations into producers of allocations

Which Business Problems Does the Tool Solve?

The challenge in today's business environment is growth. In mature domestic markets, growth is difficult because market segments in general are saturated, so you need innovation to take market share from your competitors. Otherwise, you need to generate a whole new market approach and create a market of one. Another challenge is that businesses are underpenetrated in new markets in other parts of the world. In some cases, domestic businesses have not expanded to Europe and Asia, and in others they have not properly penetrated the BRIC (Brazil, Russia, India, and China) countries.

In any case, funding growth is a question of resource allocation. Businesses must allocate resources from their existing lines of business and point them toward new areas. In order to maintain profitability, businesses have to reduce expenses in some areas to offset investments in others. The Comparative Funding Models allow managers to see the reallocation today and forecast when these new areas will begin to be self-funding.

What Else Should You Know?

The biggest consideration is underestimating the investment level you need to sufficiently fund the startup programs. You need to create a business plan for the new investment area with at least a three-year forward look. Your business plan also needs to look at all the investments – including those in product development, marketing, sales, and capital costs – required for the programs to be successful. Management needs to judge the plan and use it to set the required initial budget. Then they need to determine the businesses they will use to source the required investment.

The second consideration is how businesses can modify the plan as the years go by to reflect the changing environment, as these programs often take more time than anticipated. This, however, becomes easier year after year as your track records are established.

Case Study

Within NetCo, there is a business unit with three divisions - a "cash cow" division that has about 80% of the revenues, a smaller division that has a higher growth rate ("growth"), and a new division with the aim to go after an innovative new product space ("startup") that involves routing for cloud and mobile devices. Going into this new investment area will not be inexpensive. The business case indicates that it will require $10M in its first year, $10M in its second year, and $15 M in its third year. Given that it will take nearly a year to get to market, the first year's revenues will be zero, and the second year's revenues are estimated to be $5 M after a conservative review of the business. However, in four years, "startup" will be the second-largest and fastest-growing division in the group.

NetCo plans to fund this new division by reallocating resources from the "sources" (cash cow and growth) to the new "sink" (startup). They plan to cut the budgets of these two "source" business units by 10% (the first half through speeding up turnover and the second half through eliminating lower-priority projects). This process has four steps that they will complete in the following order:

1. From the business plan, determine the cash needs of the new sink division.
2. From a strategic look at the other profitable divisions, determine how they can fund the new business unit.
3. Model these findings over time to focus on higher-than-forecast startup expenses, as revenues will probably be later and smaller than anticipated.
4. Socialize the model with business unit managers and incorporate it into budgets, which they will review on a yearly basis.

Harnessing the Global Workforce
Outsourcing Map

What Is the Tool?

Although you may be doing more outsourced development, you probably are not doing it right. Why? Because you haven't considered how to best push the authority to outsource down to the team level, or if you have tried it and have not been successful, you have made the wrong choice in partners and need to step back and assess your decision. The Outsourcing Map will help you select the right approach for outsourcing by using a framework for evaluating options based on strategic and technical dimensions.

After you have made the decision to outsource, the challenge is to determine the best approach. In larger companies, you may be outsourcing multiple functions, including software development, product testing, payroll administration, and/or customer support. However, in large and small companies, the outsourcing decision is moving down the organization. The Outsourcing Map optimizes the choice at any level in your organization by providing you with a matrix to determine the best source of appropriate skills based on your requirements.

The Outsourcing Map is a tool consisting of a set of questions organized by strategic importance and technical difficulty, a scale to rate the answers to the questions, and a results grid.

To apply the Outsourcing Map, first answer the following questions using the scale below. You should apply this process individually to the different types of work you intend to outsource to ensure you determine the best approach for each type (e.g., outsourcing software development would produce a different Outsourcing Map than the one produced by outsourcing payroll administration).

For each question, choose the value below (1-3) that best reflects your answer:

- 1: No or low
- 2: Sometimes or medium
- 3: Yes or high

Strategic Importance

- A key component of your strategy?
- To be used over and over again in subsequent programs?
- An important part of your product's differentiation?

Technical Difficulty

- Technically sophisticated using cutting-edge components?

- Relies on internal patents or deep company know-how?

- Would like to capture the IP for future use?

Average the answers for the strategic and technical dimensions to yield two numbers from 1-3. The results of your ratings will appear on the Outsourcing Map by locating the center of a circle using the averages as X and Y coordinates. The circle will then enclose the suggested outsourcing choices.

Finally, you can improve the results of the Outsourcing Map by considering the questions below. Beyond the strategic and technical context for determining the best outsourcing approach, there are other factors that can refine your choices. Answer the following questions in order to assess the specific vendors within a given category suggested by the Outsourcing Map. Use a scale of 1-3 for each answer, but don't average the answers. Instead, use them to refine the selection in the Outsourcing Map so that you can choose between competitive options.

- A very large effort?

- A long-term effort?

- One where development cost is important?

- One where the requirements are well specified?

- Enough justification to have regional presence?

- Requires English to be spoken?

- Challenged by weak internal program management?

- One where short time-to-market is critical?

Visualization

The scorecard and the map describe the process for assessing the best form of outsourcing. The strategy and technology portions are scored from 1 (low) to 3 (high) and then averaged to help place a target circle on the Outsourcing Map, where the Strategy average value is plotted on the horizontal axis, and the Technology average value is plotted on the vertical axis.

Outsourcing Questions

Strategy	
Peripheral to the strategy or core?	1
Not used again or will be used again and again?	1
Part of differentiation?	1
Average	**1**
Technology	
How technically sophisticated?	2
How much relies on internal patents/know how?	3
Technical impact if knowledge not captured?	1
Average	**2**
"Other Factors" - refine choices after doing the overall mapping	
Small vs. large effort?	2
Long vs. short term?	2
Is cost critical?	2
Is problem well-specified?	3
Reason to have regional presence?	1
How much is English a requirement?	3
Strength of internal project management?	3
How quickly is it required?	3

Outsourcing Map

High Technology (3)	Local Resources (Silicon Valley) Ex-Employees Academic Partnerships Craigslist	Partner Specialist Joint Venture	Develop Inhouse
Medium Technology (2)	oDesk Top Coder Elance	Traditional Domestic Outsourcing Temporary Agency Partner Specialist Joint Venture	Develop Inhouse Remote Development Partner Specialist Joint Venture
Low Technology (1)	Virtual Personal Assistant Business Process Outsourcing My Man in India	Traditional Domestic Outsourcing Temporary Agency Partner Joint Venture	Remote Development
	Low Strategic Importance (1)	**Medium Strategic Importance (2)**	**High Strategic Importance (3)**

The position of the circle (Medium Technology, Low Strategy) indicates that oDesk, Top Coder and Elance are three viable choices. There are often several choices listed within a given cell. Your company should choose one based on your prior experience, specific needs, or the user interface.

What's New?

Outsourcing has spread down to the team and individual level, so it is now possible for project teams to reach out to offshore resources to accelerate their progress and increase their skillset. Given that this possibility is now available to teams, they need tools that help them address the best way to go about it. Your teams can use this decision-support model and the related graphical map to evaluate the best alternatives based on their needs.

Benefits

- Provides a **checklist of factors** to consider for selecting a partner
- **Recommends an alternative** to explore for outsourcing
- **Reduces risk** in determining the best approach to outsourcing
- Supplies real **sources of assistance** that you can apply to your project

Which Business Problems Does the Tool Solve?

This tool catalyzes action and provides a roadmap to staff up your project quickly by leveraging international resources. It takes some of the guesswork out of the process and minimizes risk by providing meaningful recommendations. Finally, it does all of this in a way that helps provide justification to management, thus speeding up approval.

What Else Should You Know?

While it is not fully possible to reduce this complex decision to a set of black-and-white rules and methods, the Outsourcing Map will help you come to a decision fast. However, you should also consider factors such as internal culture, sensitivity to intellectual property, cost, and prior experience (good or bad), which might dictate different approaches. If you are also new to outsourcing/remote development, be aware that there are a broad range of issues that can affect the quality of the resources you consider, including communication problems and resource turnover. The Outsourcing Map will help you minimize these risks. One recommendation if you are using low-cost resources on small projects is to hire two individuals at the same time to work in parallel on a small time-bound task. Then choose the one who provides the higher-quality output.

Case Study

A big transformation to automate performance approvals is taking place with the HR and IT teams at NetCo. Chuck, the IT program lead, has several time-critical tasks that will soon set the project back if he does not address them. He has been unable to secure the internal resources to accomplish three critical tasks: (1) import the past reviews from spreadsheets into the current tool; (2) change the colors and logos for a professional look; and (3) have an editor clean up the customized documentation that was created offsite and has style consistency issues. Chuck needs to drive these efforts forward, so he has turned to outsourcing to accomplish the tasks in a timely manner.

In applying the Outsourcing Map, he has answered the survey questions, confirming that an offshoring approach using some third-party hiring organization makes sense. Since the three tasks are so different, Chuck has posted three task descriptions on an outsourcing hub. He has decided to pick two graphic designers and two editors and give them a sample task before hiring the best performers. For the data-entry task, he has hired the provider with the most experience and positive ratings. Within two weeks, Chuck has added three team members to his project and, since expenses have been so low ($8K for all three tasks), only needed one sign-off.

The table above summarizes Chuck's responses to the various questions and produces an average score for the strategy and technology elements. Following the chart is the Outsourcing Map that takes the averages and plots them in a circle overlaying the map, so Chuck can see the recommended directions for the outsourcing solution.

Getting the Most Out of Social Communities
Social Community Matrix

What Is the Tool?

The use of social technology is steadily increasing and beginning to deliver real benefits in customer service, marketing, and human resources. We define social technology as the ways in which the Internet is enabling virtual communities to communicate and collaborate for the benefit of the organization. These technologies are making a material impact in ensuring that companies deliver the best products to their customers by tapping into their needs and wants. They are creating value for organizations far beyond marketing and customer support. You can use social solutions to help accelerate innovation and product development within your organization by creating a managed community where the best resources can share ideas, build on these ideas through collaboration, and escalate the best recommendations to the leadership team. While you can use such communities to address various types of issues, creating the right community with the right people for the right reason is critical to the success of the initiative. There are several third-party solutions (Spigit, Brightidea, and IBM's Jams) that are feature-rich and easily customizable to help companies quickly set up communities to engage employees and customers.

If you are just beginning to consider using communities, what is the best way to get started? The Social Community Matrix is a tool that can help you construct the most effective community for the problem you're trying to solve. This tool helps you select a solution whether you are setting up an internal community with only employees or an external community that relies on participation from the outside. Social communities have two basic organizing principles: focus and participation. These principles represent the X and Y axes of the matrix, where focus is the X axis (horizontal) and participation is the Y axis (vertical).

Focus refers to the overall objective of the community. On one hand, you can use the community in a very open-ended way to help set the direction for your company. If the questions are of this nature, then we call the community problem-focused because we are asking the members about the problems we are trying to solve. For example, what should our primary focus be for the next year? Or what technology do we need to work on today to support our five-year roadmap?

On the other hand, you can use the community to come up with specific solutions for a well-stated problem. This type of community is solution based. Example questions may include: how do we increase product performance by 30%? Or, how do we reduce product cost by 10%?

Participation refers to identifying the right members to get the best results. The most basic qualifier for participation is the degree to which it is open to those outside the community, often called an external community. It's a myth that social communities should be open to anyone with an opinion on the problem. You want to select the right members with the most informed opinions to participate in the community. This will increase the quality of the input and decrease the noise. It's a critical success factor in effectively managing the data that comes from the community.

You can apply the Social Community Matrix in the following steps:

1. Clearly define the desired outcome of the community (problem-focused vs. solution-based).

2. Determine the appropriate scope of participation (internal vs. external, narrow vs. broad).

3. Identify on the Social Community Matrix the type of community you should create to optimize your results.

Visualization

The Social Community Matrix shows how different objectives fit into a framework of community participation and focus. You select your community based on the degrees of the breadth of the community and the focus of the community - problem focused (broadly specified) or solution focused (narrowly specified).

Social Community Matrix

Benefits

- Allows you to **quickly define the right type of community** to create based on the problem
- **Accelerates product development** by increasing focus on the most important issues
- Provides an effective tool for globally dispersed organizations to **gather the collective intelligence** from their teams

Which Business Problems Does the Tool Solve?

Staying competitive requires moving faster in an increasingly complex environment. You need the best tools and technologies to keep yourself ahead of the competition and ensure that your teams are working as efficiently as possible. Few companies have the luxury of having everyone around the same conference room table to discuss issues and implement solutions. Social solutions have become increasingly important tools to ensure that companies are capturing their best ideas, effectively collaborating, and driving better decisions faster.

What Else Should You Know?

The Social Community Matrix is a high-level framework. You need to apply judgment when determining the right participants, so the selection of experts or vocal authorities should be emphasized. Social communities need to be vibrant in order to be effective. The best way to ensure their vibrancy is to have important, unique content available there, act on recommendations, and have carefully considered topics for discussion. Finally, you need to manage these social communities. It is not enough to just send out an email announcing the community and hope your members just go there. It's important to assign someone as a community manager to actively oversee the community and keep it engaging. This requires someone who is willing to make this their top priority and has at least 25% of their time available to work on it.

Case Study

NetCo has seven development centers globally dispersed across four continents, consisting of 10,000 engineers. While all the centers are executing well against the Product Roadmap, the senior leadership team does not feel they are making large enough strides in innovation. They know they have deep talent, but do not have the tools and methodologies in place to harness the best ideas, evaluate their feasibility, and then get the best ideas onto the Technology and Product Roadmaps. Bill, the EVP of engineering, has directed his team to implement a SaaS-based social software solution to create an ideation community to drive thought leadership and collaboration. Bill would also like to turn those ideas into initiatives and have the leadership team approve and fund the best recommendations.

Often, communities are given specific problems to solve over a finite time. This is called a campaign. The objective of the first campaign is to identify the top three technology initiatives that can accelerate the company's next generation of products. Bill wants to harness the best thinking and collaboration of his top architects, engineers, and technical product managers (approximately 1,000 people). Implementing the third-party tool, he invites the participants to the community, sets the campaign duration for five days, and asks them to spend 5-10% of their time on the forum, sharing their ideas, collaborating to expand others' ideas, and voting on the best ones.

At the end of the five days, Bill has reviewed the number of ideas submitted, who has been most influential in the process, and the top results of the team's efforts. He has gathered the leadership team to review the work product. They have picked three of the ideas for further investigation and given each team $25 K for expenses and a dedicated software team to flesh out their idea. Besides making it possible to inject more technology into the next generation of products, this process has increased the effective collaboration of Bill's globally dispersed team and has allowed him to build a "bottom-up" buy-in for future development initiatives.

Management

Management: Definition

There are as many definitions of management as there are of strategy (maybe even more). For this section, we will define management as "the judicious use of means to accomplish an end[1]." Many of the tools describe methods to use resources efficiently and should be helpful to those of you who are in a supervisory role. We extend the definition to include many of the actions that take place at the level in the organizational chart between the bottom and the top (those who have the title of manager or director). As a result, many of the graphical tools are oriented toward the need of the manager or director to get the most out of their organization.

Finally, the role of management spans the development lifecycle. The tools in this section also span the duration of the lifecycle, helping to make progress visible, detect problems early, and reduce risk throughout the project.

Why Is This Section Important in Supporting Innovation and Time-to-market?

Often the most difficult part of any project is getting started, which you might define as having the right set of requirements and the right set of initial plans. Without fully satisfying these two elements, you risk the loss of innovation and execution.

With innovation comes risk. In order to deliver innovative products successfully, you need to manage risk. Although it's one of the most difficult areas of management, it is one where you get the most leverage because the impact of experiencing an unplanned problem can really delay a project, so the best solution is to find a way to avoid triggering the risk in the first place. The Out-of-Bounds tools can help prevent problems from growing larger.

A risk item or an unplanned event can result in a hit to a schedule or a loss of features. The work of product development is largely invisible, so it is very hard to see how much progress your team has made. The benefit of the Risk Mind Map and Risk Management Matrix is to make the invisible visible and enable managers to anticipate risk and tangibly assess the reduction of risk over time.

Finally, there is the question, most frequent in software development, of when the product is good enough to release. Your proper management of defects at the end of the program can make the difference between a raging success and an embarrassing failure. The Bug Management Matrix can help you make better decisions at release.

Use Cases Where You Apply These Tools

In this section, the first group of graphical tools is helpful when starting a project by ensuring that you have the right requirements and an initial project plan. The second group of tools helps your teams manage risks. The third set helps management and team view the project over the lifecycle and manage exceptions if they occur. Finally, you can use the last graphical tool when the team is managing the bug-scrubbing process near shipment.

Chapter & Tool Listing

Title	Tool
Comprehensive Overview of Major Risks	Risk Mind Map
Anticipating and Mitigating Risk	Risk Management Matrix
Rapid Indicators for Early Warning	Predictive Metrics Tree
Getting Teams off to a Good Start	Nine-step Initiative Plan
Accelerating Innovative Product Definitions	Requirements Management Matrix
Project Portfolio at a Glance	PIEmatrix Multi-Project Map
Avoiding Gaps Across Functions	Function Phase Matrix
Setting Project Boundary Conditions	Boundary Conditions Diagram
How to Quickly Get Projects Back on Track	Out-of-Bounds Check
Prioritizing Defects Through the Customer's Eyes	Bug Management Matrix

[1] Merriam-Webster Dictionary, p. 706, 10th Edition, 1996

Comprehensive Overview of Major Risks
Risk Mind Map
Scott Elliott

What Is the Tool?

Product development is inherently a big set of risks. One of the main purposes of a product development process is to reduce uncertainty. Most product development teams do not adequately assess the risk factors in their programs to begin with, nor do they adequately track and manage those risks through the development process.

A fresh and graphical approach to risk assessment and management is to use a mind-mapping tool. A mind map is a way of recording a creative process where the central concern is written in the middle of the diagram and related factors are bubbles drawn off of the central bubble. Normally, mind maps are used for creative problem-solving, requirements generation, and product idea generation. However, teams can use them to brainstorm risks by leveraging a pre-populated diagram with the major risk categories (packaging, supplier, technology, reliability, etc.) and adding specific risks for the program.

Visualization

The Risk Mind Map is drawn from a real example of an optical development program. The bubble in the center is the main theme. The outer boxes are various classes of risks. The lists next to the boxes indicate some specific risks, prioritized from 1 (high) to 4 (low). Risks without numbers are the lowest priority.

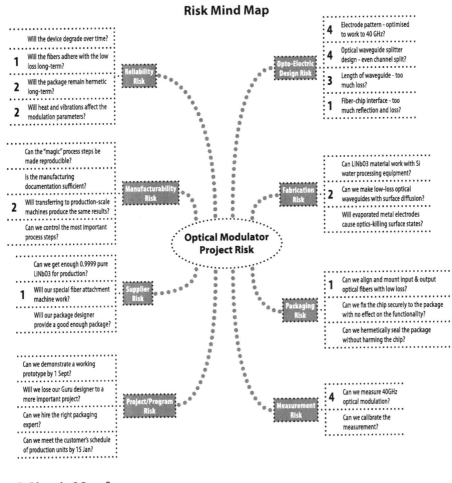

Risk Mind Map

What's New?

A set of tools that works very well for brainstorming and developing the set of risks is mind-mapping software, which replaces the old paper methods. These packages make it easy to start from a central node or idea and then add branches around the node to fill out related ideas, causes, effects, etc. Mind-mapping software also allows distributed teams to collaborate more easily that trying to do it in real time.

Benefits

- The Risk Mind Map provides an efficient method to view the **whole spectrum of risks at a glance.**
- You can see which of those risks are the most probable and/or have the **highest impact on project success.**
- You can pare and **update the risks as the project progresses.**

Which Business Problems Does the Tool Solve?

The Risk Mind Map facilitates the rapid creation of program risks by using technology that allows a distributed team to contribute to a comprehensive risk profile. The risk map allows the management team to anticipate risks sooner and prepare mitigation plans.

What Else Should You Know?

A careful and credible risk analysis needs time and open, honest team communication. Often, the highest-risk parts of the project are not immediately evident until you do some structured thinking and brainstorming, as illustrated by the case study below. The quality of the Risk Mind Map is highly dependent on people, so you should ensure that the most experienced team members participate. If the team lacks depth, supplement the team by creating the Risk Mind Map with principal engineers or architects from other teams.

Case Study

NetCo hired the brightest PhD engineers to develop a state-of-the-art product. For them, the challenge and fun were in designing the advanced networking product utilizing optical components for switching. Although this had never been done (at the time), the engineers were virtually 100% sure they could do it successfully in the allotted one-year time because they had made similar designs in other labs and were confident in their computer models. They couldn't wait to see their names on the groundbreaking technical papers.

The process starts with the team brainstorming risks in the product development project. The first step is to list the major categories such as product definition, technology, competition, commercialization, support, reliability, etc. Next, they add branches to the major categories in order to identify all of the foreseeable risk elements for their specific project. Then they cut off any branches with a very low probability, such as "lab hit by meteor." A typical project Risk Mind Map will identify 30 to 50 such possible risks on the full map. Of the 30-50 risks in the outer branches, the team should then identify which are the most likely and would have the highest impact.

After building out and prioritizing the branches of the Risk Mind Map, it is time to make assignments to validate the risks and propose mitigations. A team member, subgroup, or third party should study each high-priority or high-impact risk. For example, someone in the finance department might assess the financial risks.

The project manager owns this risk management process. The Risk Mind Map and the Gantt schedule are the two most important graphical tools of their job. A best practice is to have a real or virtual "war room" where the project manager posts this map prominently, usually on the company wiki or internal collaboration software. For software development, they could use a similar map as a "bug list."

As the team mitigates or eliminates risks, they should edit and re-prioritize them on the Risk Mind Map and other project tools like the Gantt chart. New risks can (and will) appear and should be added. The team should communicate the Risk Mind Map to all stakeholders regularly. They should make a "snapshot" of the Risk Mind Map at least weekly.

At the end of the project, the team should use these snapshots of the Risk Mind Map to do a retrospective. How well did they anticipate and mitigate the risks? What did they learn, and what can they build into the product development process to make it smoother and faster for the next project?

When they did the risk analysis, it became clear that the greatest risks (#1 and #2 in the figure) were in the much less glamorous area of getting optical fibers to align and stick to the ends of the chip and stay there permanently. The project leader boldly decided to put 80% of the team on this aspect of the project, much to the initial disappointment of the gurus. The project leader allowed them to spend most of their time on the modulator design only after they had demonstrated 90% confidence that the fiber alignment and attachment process would work - a subproject that took nine months! In just three more months, they had a fully functional and reliable product ready for the market! Had the team not done this thorough risk analysis and mitigation effort, the project would have taken much longer.

Anticipating and Mitigating Risk
Risk Management Matrix

What Is the Tool?

The Risk Management Matrix is an elegant way to anticipate, manage, and mitigate product development risks. A common myth is that you can't take the risk out of invention. But, in reality, you can significantly reduce risk even in the most inventive programs by anticipating it. The best way to implement this tool for risk reduction is to use the entire cross-functional team to forecast risk using the Risk Mind Map. The benefit of this methodology is that there is a specific risk trigger point (a quantitative threshold), as well as a mitigating action plan if you exceed that threshold. When combined together, they make this approach more effective than the more subjective approaches. However, you can use the subjective Risk Mind Map approach as the front end for the Risk Management Matrix, combining the best of both tools.

The matrix consists of a list of risks versus criteria and assumptions. The risks themselves are in the first column and act as headers for each row, which teases apart each risk. The column headings consist of risk attributes such as likelihood, consequence, and measure. The likelihood and consequence are on scales of one to ten, with one being essentially impossible and zero impact respectively. The remaining headings are the risk threshold, the date by which the threshold should be equaled, and, finally, a short phrase that outlines the action plan.

The cross-functional team creates the matrix in a workshop fashion. The project manager usually leads the session and plans ahead by creating a draft of the matrix, listing some of the likely risks and filling out the rest of the attributes and risk management factors. The project manager can often derive those risks from the list of boundary review conditions. The creation of this matrix should take place during the first 10-15% of a project's duration.

After creating the tool, you can use it on an ongoing basis by quickly reviewing it at the weekly team meetings. The goal is to walk through any of the critical metrics, add new metrics as they occur, and remove the old ones if their risk has been eliminated. When a trigger point occurs, it is time to review the action plan and put remediation in gear. Based on new knowledge, you may update and modify it. The secret, however, is to act and not wait for "things to get better" on their own because they rarely do.

Visualization

The Risk Management Matrix is an example table that lists various risks, their overall impact, and then an action plan if the risk values are exceeded. The "impact" and "likelihood" columns are on scales from 1 to 10, where 1 indicates zero risk and absolutely no impact on the project. A rating of 5 in the case of impact means that the risk has one-half of the largest negative impact conceivable, such as a one-month slip for a nine-month program. Similarly, a 5 on the likelihood scale means one-half of the typical likelihood, which would be on the order of 50%. The benefit of the matrix is that trigger points (thresholds) and action plans are created at the beginning of the program where you have the most clarity, not during the occurence of the risk when judgement tends to be clouded.

The "metric" is the measurable quantity associated with the risk. The "threshold" is the value you must hit by the time you ship (unless otherwise stated). The "date" is the time by which the performance must equal or exceed the threshold value unless it is the date by which you are monitoring the metric. Finally, the "action plan" column indicates the high-level objectives of an action plan. It may refer to a much more detailed action plan, which should be sufficiently described so that a reader of the Risk Management Matrix has a sense of what will take place if you trigger a threshold.

Risk Management Matrix								
Status	Risk	Impact	Likelihood	Metric	Threshold	Current Value	Date	Action Plan
	Global team does not communicate frequently enough. Want to keep weekly communication high.	4	7	Meetings per week	2	2.5	Current	Invoke team's elevation plan, purchase videoconferencing systems, change incentives
	Data captured on long forms from online interaction sessions must not be lost if user gets error message or returns to screen.	6	6	% Data Lost	10%	25%	Q3 FY 13	Design review current forms layout, bring in Expert Co. consulting firm, change staff balance
	Server must respond to users rapidly under fairly high loads - expect page to be updated way under a second.	7	7	Ms at 1000 Users	259	1000	Q2 FY 13	Add architect and create tiger team with system optimization experience
	Financial partner cooperation is critical to this household finance program, and we need to have a sufficient number at launch.	4	6	Institutions	1000	247	Q3 FY 13	Increase business development staff, change incentive compensation, add external business development firm
	Mobile operating system support must be in place at the same time as launching the desktop version.	5	6	On Time	Q4 FY-14	Q4 FY-14	Current	Track schedule prediction accuracy. If slip then recruit internal team from Vietnam (permission already granted)

What's New?

The new parts of this approach are the use of quantitative trigger points and the creation of an action plan in the clear light of sanity far before the red lights start flashing when you have to deal with a problem. In addition, by including the entire team (typically five to 15) in the formation of the Risk Reduction Matrix, you get a more robust matrix and team buy-in as a by-product.

Benefits

- **You can identify risks** before they occur.
- There is a reduction of risk impact due to **early detection**.
- You will **have quantitative metrics** that help clarify when to act on a risk item.
- **Accelerated actions** will happen because of the clear thresholds and the agreement to follow the process.

Which Business Problems Does the Tool Solve?

You might consider risk management the evil twin sister of innovation. Ultimately a break from the past, innovation inherently brings with it additional risks, which you can still manage. One way to manage those risks is through micromanagement, but this obviously quenches innovation. The other way, consistent with the increasing desire to delegate authority and empower teams, is to have the team manage risks on their own.

From a larger business perspective, having a risk management system in place helps improve project execution because it can help the team anticipate, prevent, and mitigate risks. Such risks can result in delays or additional project expenses. Unfortunately, while the team solves these problems, the schedule marches on and the project expenses accumulate.

What Else Should You Know?

The Risk Reduction Matrix is only as good as the inputs in its initial formulation. Teams often add one or two principal engineers for this exercise to help them come up with a deeper, more comprehensive, and more thoughtful list of risks. While it is important to have the right people and follow a process to fill out the matrix, the assignment of values to likelihood and consequence (or impact) can get out of hand. It is important that you mainly try to identify the high- and medium-impact risks that can possibly happen. If you get stuck in assigning values, try pairwise comparison and cross-check the values you assigned.

The seduction of optimism is probably the biggest risk in the application of this tool. Don't be a "prisoner of hope" because there is an often false belief that the risk will just go away on its own or will be worn down by working harder. Make sure that when a risk trigger is crossed, you take action immediately. Remember when you had a clear perspective at the beginning of the project? What has changed? It is likely that nothing has really changed except that you are now under pressure to deliver and have many issues to worry about, so you don't want to worry about this problem.

Case Study

WebCo is about to kick off a multi-site next-generation home finance project that leverages all of the geographies in important ways (and for the first time). Brian, the project manager, and Molly, the product manager, got together after agreeing on the importance of doing a risk management exercise. Their first step was to create a rough draft of the Risk Reduction Matrix. This draft involved Brian and Molly, who listed the top risks using the Risk Mind Map. They also estimated the likelihood and consequence ratings. Using this as a starting place, they called a team meeting with a global teleconference and invited two architects to participate as well.

The team reviewed Brian's and Molly's initial work before the meeting and came prepared. After an hour and a half, they listed the following risks on this initial round: team communication, server responsiveness, data integrity, usability, and financial partnership agreements. The initial table had the following trigger metrics and values: meeting frequency (2x per week), server responsiveness (250ms with a load of 100 users), screen data integrity (100% of screen data acquired no matter what error message), and financial partner signup frequency (15 partners signed per week).

The project team put the matrix on their wiki site and reviewed it on a weekly basis. Although we don't know yet how the matrix impacted the project's final outcome, we can say that, six weeks into the project's design phase, the requirements for the home finance software included mobile device compatibility as well. The team added this requirement to the Risk Management Matrix after they had an Out-of-Bounds Check, which would impact the schedule unless resources were added to the team. We can say that both the matrix and weekly review have kept the team's communication sufficient for this new global approach and ensured that the new mobile requirement is on schedule.

Rapid Indicators for Early Warning

Predictive Metrics Tree

What Is the Tool?

Companies are measuring the wrong things and ending up with the wrong results. Many times we get stuck on measuring what's easy instead of what's useful, or we focus on validating whether we succeeded or failed instead of measuring the elements that would tell us when a project is getting ready to go out of bounds. Predictive metrics are the solution to this problem, and the Predictive Metrics Tree is the tool that helps ensure you're measuring the right actions to achieve your program goals.

It provides a direct line of sight between the project goal and the three to five key metrics that, when defined and frequently measured, will best predict the likelihood of achieving the desired goal. Predictive metrics are fundamentally different from results metrics in that, instead of measuring an outcome, the organization measures a process or behavior that drives the result. The reason it is called a tree is that the diagram is a hierarchy with goals at the top and branches coming down from the goals, so it visually looks like a tree.

The Balanced Scorecard[1] was a revolutionary concept that brought needed attention to non-financial metrics to help executives get a more comprehensive view of their business. The Predictive Metrics Tree is different from the Balanced Scorecard since the Predictive Metrics Tree is derived from a root cause analysis of barriers to the company achieving their objectives, rather than a pre-populated (balanced) list of financial and non-financial metrics.

Constructing a Predictive Metrics Tree is a cross-functional group process that the leadership team typically carries out. The critical aspect of constructing predictive metrics is to ensure, with all the complexity associated with delivering a product to market, that the team is sharply focused on the three to five elements that will have the biggest impact on whether or not you will achieve the overall program goal. This process consists of crisply defining these elements and the key drivers of these elements. Having created drivers, it is easy to come up with initiatives and metrics that monitor progress. The last step is frequently measuring and managing the resulting predictive metrics.

Project Goal: The cross-functional team will define the goal of the project. Typical examples in product development include delivering a project against a specific schedule, cost quality, and revenue targets. The project goal is a shared objective that is time-bound and measurable. The team derives the goal from a broader organizational and/or corporate goal. This is the result metric that the team typically measures, as opposed to the predictive metrics we are discussing in this chapter.

Key Drivers: The team derives key drivers from the project goal. Once the project team establishes a goal, they will identify the three to five key actions that will have the greatest impact on successfully achieving that goal. It is important that the team bound the number of drivers to ensure that they can sharpen their focus on high-impact areas and avoid the ineffective method of "measuring everything."

Initiatives: The initiatives are the key actions within each driver that will ensure that the team achieves their goal. By identifying the key initiative within each driver, the project team continues to narrow their focus to gain clarity on the most relevant actions or behaviors that will drive the successful outcome of the stated goal.

Predictive Metrics: The predictive metrics are the processes or behaviors that measure progress to the goal. For each initiative, the project team will identify one measurable parameter as the best indicator of progress. It is critical that the team accurately define each predictive metric with detailed definitions, frequency of collection, units of measurement, and target values.

Once the team defines a suite of three to five predictive metrics, they should track them on a daily or weekly basis. The team can typically do this in the weekly project team review or in a weekly management review. They typically construct a predictive metrics dashboard as a single presentation slide and include it in the review. These metrics give the team the best chance of identifying whether there is progress toward the stated goal and allow them to take quick action to rectify any identified issues.

Visualization

The Predictive Metrics Tree is a hierarchical diagram that breaks a goal down to key drivers, initiatives to manage the drivers, and the associated metrics for each initiative. The example shown below is drawn from a startup where typical challenges are detailed, including release schedule, staffing, sales and cash.

Predictive Metrics Tree

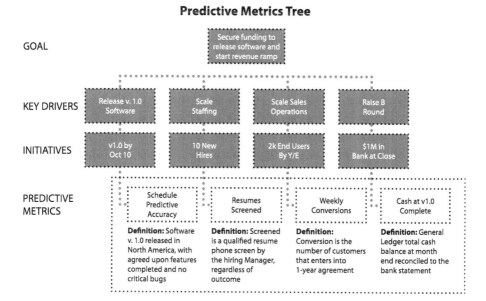

GOAL	Secure funding to release software and start revenue ramp			
KEY DRIVERS	Release v. 1.0 Software	Scale Staffing	Scale Sales Operations	Raise B Round
INITIATIVES	v1.0 by Oct 10	10 New Hires	2k End Users By Y/E	$1M in Bank at Close
PREDICTIVE METRICS	Schedule Predictive Accuracy	Resumes Screened	Weekly Conversions	Cash at v1.0 Complete
	Definition: Software v. 1.0 released in North America, with agreed upon features completed and no critical bugs	**Definition:** Screened is a qualified resume phone screen by the hiring Manager, regardless of outcome	**Definition:** Conversion is the number of customers that enters into 1-year agreement	**Definition:** General Ledger total cash balance at month end reconciled to the bank statement

The metrics summarized in the chart above are:

Schedule Prediction Accuracy Metric - measures schedule deviation against the planned schedule using the formula (Actual Schedule - Predicted Schedule/Predicted Schedule), target under 10% .

Résumés Screened Metric - number of candidates screened via phone screen, target above 10.

Weekly Conversion Rate Metric - number of prospects turned into customers who enter a one-year agreement per week; target 40 per week.

Estimated Cash at Close - predicted cash at the closing of the next round, target $1M or more in the bank.

To further illustrate, examine the predictive metric "Résumés Screened." Many managers would be tempted to measure the initiative "10 New Hires" with the metric "number of new hires this week or month", which is not predictive or useful. Alternatively, if you measure the number of Résumés Screened, then you have an early indication of whether or not you're going to hit the goal of your initiative (10 New Hires). As you measure this predictive metric on a weekly (or more frequent) basis, you can quickly reinforce with the hiring manager to budget time to screen résumés. Over time, you can set targets for the number of résumés that you'll need to screen to hit the goal of the initiative.

What's New?

The notion of the Balanced Scorecard is fundamentally flawed. Why does it matter if your metrics are balanced? What matters most is that the metrics help management to focus on the critical parameters that deliver success. Furthermore, most balanced score systems are lag indicators that are like "driving while looking through the rear view mirror." Companies are measuring the wrong things and ending up with the wrong results.

Benefits

- **Increased confidence** that this early warning system will provide the best opportunity to get a project back on track.
- With an early indication that a program is heading for trouble, the leadership team can make **data-based decisions**.
- **Measuring things that matter** — not just what is easy to measure.
- Measuring three to five elements instead of dozens allows the project leadership to **focus on the most critical areas**.

Which Business Problems Does the Tool Solve?

A Predictive Metrics Tree is one of the best process management tools to achieve your objectives. The predictive nature of these metrics allows managers and their teams to see where they really stand and where they are headed relative to target, and to continually optimize the approach. The Predictive Metrics Tree helps align the organization and reduce waste because all the initiatives are coordinated and ultimately tied to the overall objective.

What Else Should You Know?

Coming up with the predictive metrics is not easy, but, if you follow the process where initiatives are derived from goals, the guesswork will be minimized. You should also test the quality of the metric by verifying that it may change in a material way in less than two weeks. Finally, ask others outside your team if they are convinced that the predictive metrics you have identified will address 80% or more of the issues that will ensure your success.

Case Study

The startup CleanCo has secured funding to deliver the 1.0 release of their product. They understand that the next round of funding after the round they have just received will be based on four key drivers: (1) release the software; (2) scale the technical staff; (3) scale sales operations; and (4) raise the next round of funding. The Predictive Metrics Tree provides a direct line of sight between the corporate goal (shipping the 1.0 release) and the predictive metrics that will allow the management team to visualize any early warning signs that would prevent the team from achieving their goal. Review the model above and see how each predictive metric ties to the corporate goal.

In each case, the company has clearly defined the predictive metric and should measure and review it on a frequent basis (in this case weekly). They can track all four of these metrics on a spreadsheet and update them in a matter of minutes.

---

[1] R. S. Kaplan and D. P. Norton, "The Balanced Scorecard - Measures that Drive Performance," Harvard Business Review, January 1992

Getting Teams Off to a Good Start

Nine-step Initiative Plan

What Is the Tool?

Sometimes it is necessary for you to personally take charge and attack problems that drain your organization's innovation or to remove obstacles that impede rapid cycle time. The Nine-step Initiative Plan is a powerful starting point that leads teams through improvement projects by laying out the basic steps in order to get them started quickly. Successful improvement projects require individuals to be aligned, have a common vision, and know how they will measure success. You can use this outline of steps to help you get started more quickly.

Nine-step Initiative Plan process:

1. Form core team
2. Review charter statement
3. Establish process and results metrics and verify availability of resources to reach targets
4. Identify alternatives by gathering best-in-company and best-in-class data
5. Develop a list of key process activities
6. Design deployment materials
7. Conduct pilot deployment
8. Standardize process for broader implementation
9. Monitor metrics for training, deployment, and effective use

Each project should have a sponsor or team lead who can select the right people, charter the team, provide a clear definition of success, and time-bound the effort (when the project needs to be completed and how much time team members should budget). You can use this structure as a guideline and customize it based on the needs of the project (e.g., you may choose to use only seven of the steps). The best approach is to create an initial draft that represents your best thinking in the relevant steps of the process and then modify it as needed.

Completing the process can take two to three one-hour meetings. It's important to time-bound this effort to ensure that you move from planning to doing, as you can make changes on the fly after you have started.

Visualization

The Nine-step Initiative Plan lists the nine steps to successfully implement a large scale change management program. The second column contains bullets summarizing the step and the third column describes an example application which is detailed in the case study paragraph to follow.

Nine-step Initiative Plan	
1 Form core team	
• Set schedule guidelines • Ensure the right team composition • Rough out schedule and time requirements	Sanjiv, the CEO, assigns four people to develop the Concept Check-in process: Brad (program manager), Maureen (product manager), Sarah (HW development manager), and Jake (industrial design lead). The team agrees to prioritize this activity and invest 4-6 hours to complete the nine-step process.
2 Review charter statement	
• Reach a consensus on the charter • Develop a buy-in strategy • Begin a buy-in process • Revise the charter as needed	The core team is chartered with developing and piloting a new Concept Check-in process, including training the cross-functional team. The team will develop the check-in template and provide a completed example of a high-quality document. The objective of the check-in is to create a scalable process that supports the growing organization in early project decision-making and team alignment.
3 Establish process and results metrics and verify availability of resources	
• Establish the desirable behavioral change • Brainstorm predictive metrics	The best way to manage change is to measure behavior. To ensure the organization is embracing this change, the core team has come up with the following metrics: • Process metrics: % teams trained and % teams that use the template for the review (target 90%) • Results metrics: % teams presenting the completed template at the review (target 90%)
4 Identify alternatives by gathering best-in-company and best-in-class data	
• Get examples from the prior experience of the team and constituents • List pros and cons of each best practice • Identify key elements from best-in-company and best-in-class data	• Brad is assigned the task of identifying existing process information that could be leveraged for the effort. • Maureen is tasked with researching industry best practices for similar reviews. • All team members share best practices from previous experience.

5	**Develop a list of key process activities**	
	• Develop a high-level block list • Identify template options • Document the key activities	The team has created a four- to six-page PowerPoint document that serves as a template for the Concept Check-in. It contains the following data: • Project overview: target market, key features, gross margin target, project team, and ID sketches • Project schedule: high-level major milestones • Key issues/risks • High-level financials

6	**Design deployment materials**	
	• Outline and document key process components • Review the components with key stakeholders • Obtain management approval	Once the Concept Check-in template has been developed, the core team reviews it with key stakeholders. Once feedback has been incorporated, the team is ready to pilot it on a real project.

7	**Conduct pilot deployment**	
	• Develop consistent development process documentation (second draft) • Perform the process on one project • Gain management approval	Based on the product roadmap, the best candidate for the pilot is the mid-range Widget X. Brad is the program manager for this project, so he leads the training with the rest of the cross-functional team. When the team completes the preparation of the template, Brad schedules a Concept Check-in with the leadership team. Feedback from the review has led the team to improve the process prior to the broader rollout.

8	**Standardize process for broader implementation**	
	• Revise the feedback from the pilot • Define the implementation plan • Create documentation • Conduct initial seminars for functional management and staff • Refine deployment as needed	The core team identifies 40 people in the organization that would require training on the Concept Check-in process. Two training sessions are conducted using the Widget X project as an example. The core team makes additional refinements to the Concept Check-in training materials based on the broader rollout. Training materials are then posted on the company wiki for future reference.

9	**Monitor metrics for training, deployment, and effective use**	
	• Reflect on the nine-step process • Recognize the team and other contributors	The core team monitors the following success metrics: • % trained on the process • % projects that hold a Concept Check-in • % using the template at the Concept Check-in These serve as a baseline to ensure the team is seeing the expected behavioral change in the organization.

What's New?

What's new is this high-impact process that will ensure that teams quickly establish a firm foundation from which they can successfully execute their projects or improvement programs. Typically, organizations do not have a standard methodology for starting up new teams, but they would really benefit from one.

Benefits

- ⊙ You get new **initiatives off to a solid start** by gaining clarity on objectives.
- ⊙ You **accelerate programs** by piloting new processes prior to broader implementation.
- ⊙ You **establish clear success criteria** to drive trade-offs and measure progress throughout the program.
- ⊙ You **minimize "restarts"** caused by unclear requirements.

Which Business Problems Does the Tool Solve?

There is no time for wasted effort. By creating a standardized set of steps to get a cross-functional team going, you can reduce the time wasted at the beginning of improvement projects. This is important since most of us don't have much experience in improvement initiatives. In addition, by starting with a tested template, you minimize the probability of first-time errors.

What Else Should You Know?

Having an initial project plan is only a starting point. It is not a plan you slavishly follow without examination. It is a mistake to have only the project manager doing this (although it is OK for the project manager to get things started). Finally, if you have any steps that are more than one week apart, then you do not have a finely tuned plan and you need to add more detail.

Case Study

WebCo is expanding their product line and has ramped up hiring to ensure that they can execute their business plan. With many new people in the company and parallel development projects, the leadership team wants to implement an early product review process. Their objective is to ensure that teams get off to the best possible start to achieve their market introduction and revenue goals. The CEO has asked a small team of people to create the process and be responsible for rolling it out throughout the organization. The goal is to create consistency across the teams so that the process can best support early project decision making and team alignment. The core team will use the Nine-step Initiative Plan to architect the product review process, and will use the Product Roadmap to identify the pilot for the process before they roll it out throughout the company.

Accelerating Innovative Product Definitions
Requirements Management Matrix

What Is the Tool?

Innovation often rests on the creativity used in the product definition stage of a program. This best practice lifts the essential elements of the sprint-based development methodology (agile) and applies it to the front end of product development, often called the concept or definition phase. The essence of agile development is turning user stories into code and testing them with a proxy for the customer. Each cycle is called a sprint, with the goal of doing as many use cases (or user stories) as possible in each sprint.

You can compile the use cases into a list of scenarios and manage this list by applying a Kanban process. The term "Kanban" comes from the Japanese quality system pioneered by Toyota, where you work on a "just-in-time" basis as the system provides inputs for each phase just when you need them[1]. You can apply this system in the requirements process by starting with your initial list of scenarios (inventory) of unfinished requirements, defining them creatively and innovatively (requirement by requirement), and tracking them one by one. For example, if you have 10 use cases that product management has defined as critical to the product, you focus on the metrics, the number of undefined use cases, and the number of defined use cases. Both defined and undefined use cases are tracked because, often in the requirements process, new use cases are added as new scenarios are envisioned.

By applying a sprint-like agile process to requirements definition, the management team works alongside the development team to select, refine, and document requirements. The management team does not have to be co-located with the development team, but they should have frequent contact. The team can initiate the sprint process by taking a one-page concept definition that product marketing proposes and a representative of the management team (typically the VP of marketing or CMO) shapes. They can bring this concept definition into a work session with the core team (four to six members including quality and user experience) and the management team (three to five C-level managers who oversee the business unit).

The outcome of the work session is a refined and extended product concept description. The team breaks the set of requirements into three groups – Candidate, In Process, and Defined. The Candidate requirements are those that the team plans to discuss, while the In Process requirements are those the team has presented, but has not yet finished (or on which they have not reached full agreement). The team goes off and works on the open requirements and iterates the definition with the customer representative. In no more than two weeks from the first session, the team gets back together and reviews the Candidate and In Process requirements, with the goal of converting all of those into Defined in one or two more sessions. This process typically repeats one more time, and then the project is at a point where it can move into development.

Visualization

The two charts below show how agile development concepts are applied to product definition. The first chart is an example Requirements Management Matrix that lists the maturity of some example requirements for a case study project of putting in place a new human resource system. The candidate requirements are initial use cases that are potential requirements, the In Process column shows what requirements are being detailed and carefully defined, and the third column lists all the requirements that have been fully defined and accepted. This snapshot from the end of the first session indicates only two defined requirements. By session three, the number of defined requirements should be 10, as shown by the line graph below. The vertical axis is the number of undefined requirements and the horizontal axis is the session number.

Requirements Management Matrix (After First Session)		
Candidate	**In Process**	**Defined**
1. 360 Feedback	1. Union/Non-Union compatible	1. SAAS
2. Salary Benchmarks	2. Pre-populated feedback sentences	2. Corrective Action
3. Calibration	3. Tracking of last year's performance	
	4. Goal setting	
	5. Performance Improvement	

The team derived the table above from the Kanban manufacturing process (just in time). There are three columns in the table, which shows the status of the requirements at a given snapshot in time. This is the snapshot of the project after the first definition session (also reflected in the chart below at the second data point). The first column describes the requirements that the team knows about, but has not yet defined. The second column lists those requirements they have discussed, but have not finished. The last column represents the requirements they have agreed upon and fully defined.

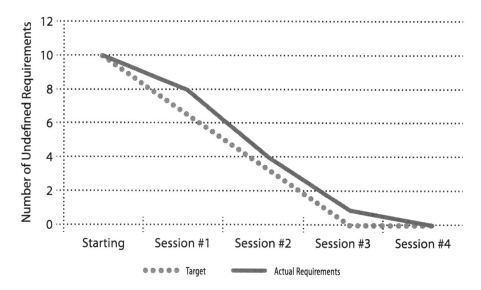

Burn Down of Outstanding Requirements

The chart above shows the progression or burn down of undefined requirements over time. The vertical axis is the number of undefined requirements, and the horizontal line is the session number. The ideal chart would start with the total number of undefined requirements (all of them) on the left and then slope down to zero by the third session. This burn down chart gives the team members a sense of progress and helps them focus on completing quality definitions as soon as possible.

What's New?

With the trends toward Web 2.0, software as a service, and cloud-based computing, there is a need to support a very rapid development cycle (often measured in weeks, not months), with a key focus on the front end where you have the core feature set defined. It is possible to borrow some of the best practices from agile software development and apply them to the management/team interface. This yields an approach where the management team (or a subset) works collaboratively with the development team to define the product in real time and innovate in a real hurry, which can result in the definition of a large product in four to six weeks and draw out the best thinking from the organization. "Fast and good" is possible.

Benefits

- This methodology can help you create **compelling product definitions**.

- It **increases definition speed** because of the tight loop of iteration between development and management.

- The quality of the definition is better because we **have the collective intelligence** of the organization.

- The management team will tend to bring more cross-functional requirements into play, thereby ensuring that they have **"total product" defined**, not just the core feature set.

Which Business Problems Does the Tool Solve?

Poor and changing product definition is the number one reason for delays in projects. This is also where innovation takes place. This technique helps break the myth that you cannot have both innovation and speed at the same time, since this process facilitates innovative requirements and tracks them. The most important benefit of this method is that it helps organizations develop really difficult platform programs quickly since they are often clean sheet and their requirements are very open-ended and unconstrained. It also has the side benefit of creating a common vision for the product, which really helps downstream when you need to make further tradeoffs.

What Else Should You Know?

Management involvement with the development team is not a substitute for direct customer interaction. Be sure to find ways to interview or interact with potential customers. Collecting requirements directly from the customer (and channel partners) is as necessary here as it is in any development system. This is also resource intensive, so most organizations would be too stressed to have all projects in development follow this method. In this case, the executive team may need to flag projects that have attributes well-suited to this method (large scope, platforms involving subsystems, new to the world, or new to the company).

Case Study

NetCo was planning to roll out a new employee rating and evaluation system next fall. The design team - consisting of Chuck (the IT program lead), Betty (the VP of HR), and Richard (the leader of the project management group) - conducted three requirement-collecting workshops across the country. In addition, they created an "as-is" and "to-be" process design and a set of recommendations to management. However, after the third management review and six months of work, they seemed no closer than when they started. The head of one of the businesses suggested the agile management approach because they saw how effective it was in helping their division in product development.

The same person agreed to work closely with the design team. In a matter of six weeks, by the end of the third meeting, there was complete agreement on the holistic vision of the project. At that point, they drafted a statement of work and used it to find the software vendor and integration partners. They concluded the definition phase of the project and started the formal development phase. The IT program lead described this as one of the fastest recoveries of any project he had worked on and indicated that, given the top management participation, the requirements were likely to stick.

[1] Hiranabe, Kenji Visualizing Agile Projects using Kanban Boards
http://www.infoq.com/articles/agile-kanban-boards, accessed November, 2011

Project Portfolio at a Glance

PIEmatrix Multi-Project Map

Paul Dandurand

What Is the Tool?

PIEmatrix™ is a web-based platform that companies can deploy across their organizations' functional areas, such as engineering, human resources, product marketing, sales, finance, and operations, to represent the cross-functional implications of a program. It's visually easy for non-project experts and, therefore, friendly to people outside of product development and IT.

In new product development (NPD) functions, projects are iterative in that, after you complete one project, you then go at it again with a follow-up product and so on. In addition, organizations that have short time-to-market need processes that are very similar from one project to another to be efficient. Because these types of projects are repetitive in nature, companies can establish standard processes for execution that drive effectiveness. PIEmatrix helps to tie processes to projects and allow standardization.

These repeatable processes would include common phases, steps, roles, and deliverable file templates. Furthermore, since all projects are relatively complex, they can have multiple process streams that run in parallel. For example, an NPD lifecycle could have the first process for project management, the second for product ideation, prototyping, and development, and a third for compliance preparation and regulatory auditing. Teams can do all of these in parallel across the phases of the project's lifecycle.

The PIEmatrix model visually displays these process streams as stackable layers and the phases of the lifecycle as pie slices, hence the name "PIEmatrix". "PIE" represents the top-view slices like those of a pizza pie, and "matrix" represents the layers that intersect the slices like flipping the pie onto its side and seeing the cheese, sauce, and crust in each slice. Teams can view the layering of the stacked processes as subprojects. This makes it easy for certain team members to visually focus on their own subproject (process layer) during execution without being overwhelmed by the entire complexity of the overall project or program.

PIEmatrix has a dashboard that visually displays the project pies graphically on a single page, showing progress and milestone indicators in real time. The color codes show the progress of different states. The graphic below represents the states in gray scale, while the actual tool uses the following codes: Dark green represents what is completed, and light green means in progress. Yellow means risk (check it out before it gets worse), and red means trouble (solve me today).

Finally, PIEmatrix is for all the people working on or having some stake in the project. It has easy-to-follow steps with knowledge tips for assigned work. There is a built-in team collaboration system with messaging and email notifications. It also provides personal to-do lists and calendar pages for a quick view of what's hot on your plate this week.

Visualization

Below is a generic visualization of a stack of five projects in a five-phase project management system. The Axis project represents an initiative to capture post-mortem project data across the company using a project-history approach. The Axis project has an issue because the focus groups are not complete yet (dark indicator), and the Star CRM project does not have requirements yet (dark indicator). Otherwise, all the projects are running without issues. The Polaris project is in some trouble because it is behind schedule. The Finance Integration project, which aims to train all project managers how to create project budgets, is ahead and has completed 90% of the Define slice (phase).

PIEmatrix Multi-Project Map

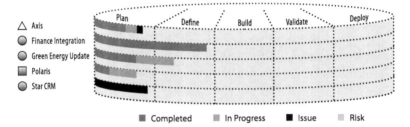

Legend	
△	Axis
●	Finance Integration
●	Green Energy Update
▢	Polaris
●	Star CRM

■ Completed   ▦ In Progress   ■ Issue   ▨ Risk

What's New?

What's new is that PIEmatrix takes a process and visual focus on project management. The approach is not task-focused like other traditional tools, but rather drives the right path for a successful project outcome with better processes. The PIEmatrix approach calls out other sub-processes with an emphasis on the how and not the what. For example, rather than having a series of deliverables and associated tasks around product definition, the overall process would include the how-to for each of the sub-processes for the voice of the customer, requirements translation, and product specifications.

These processes are also easy to update. You simply upload them to the PIEmatrix server, and all subsequent projects that flow through the system will use the new and updated processes. This makes process improvement very rapid and natural.

Benefits

- ◉ **Creates a learning organization** that adopts best practices very quickly.
- ◉ **Increases efficiency** because it provides a lightweight process framework.
- ◉ **Produces effectiveness** since the work you do has the right steps for success.
- ◉ Allows management to simultaneously **see the big picture** and dive into the details.
- ◉ Provides an **executive dashboard** for project reporting.

Which Business Problems Does the Tool Solve?

This tool solves many business problems that have prevented companies from getting innovative products to market more quickly. PIEmatrix directly addresses the age-old problem of repeating mistakes (and the lack of organizational learning).

The PIEmatrix structure is perfect for process streams on large projects where different groups focus on different processes, yet are still dependent on each other. The layers of pies that comprise the total project clearly represent the cross-functional dependencies, which make it easy for management to see where there are possible breakdowns and act before they occur.

Finally, because it is easy to incorporate new learning into the PIEmatrix framework, it encourages teams to do so. Since all teams use the same model, they must always adopt new learning. Knowledge dissemination is instantaneous.

What Else Should You Know?

Implementation of a system this comprehensive can have risks if you have not done the upfront investment properly. It's recommended that you do a targeted quick-win project first in a contained group (functional). This presents a focus on what to target for the first process. Expect a fair amount of time to be invested in building complex, key processes. Teams can then add more complexity to the process over time. The PIEmatrix real-time dynamic deployment feature makes it really easy to enhance the best-practice process continuously over time.

If the organization has a high degree of process sophistication with documented processes, then this is not a large barrier. However, if an organization is not accustomed to process management, it will require some effort (and behavior change) for them to deploy PIEmatrix across the enterprise.

Most importantly, it takes leadership to instill a culture of discipline, recover from stumbles, and continue the path toward improvement. Having top leadership support is essential for success.

Case Study

NetCo was using this tool in their engineering department to manage employee-training programs around the world to help solidify the recently installed global development process. The key problem was that employee turnover (changing to new jobs, shifting out of engineering, or leaving the company) had a significant impact on the consistency of training quality to engineers and managers. The firm chose PIEmatrix to help capture the organizational knowledge and minimize the impact of the loss of knowledge as people moved on.

Avoiding Gaps Across Functions
Function Phase Matrix

What Is the Tool?

The Function Phase Matrix allows a cross-functional project team to identify project objectives, roles and responsibilities, and key deliverables across the phases of a project. Although it is typically the responsibility of the program manager, it is best to create the Function Phase Matrix as a team exercise to allow cross-disciplinary discussion on potential gaps or overlaps between the functions. You can use the matrix to visually identify dependencies between team members and milestone deliverables.

Visualization

The Function Phase Matrix is a table organized by key functions (rows) and project phases (columns), indicating the activities that require completion during that phase. This provides an overview of the entire development process in a one-page view. It is very useful for helping define roles and responsibilities at the beginning of a project.

Function Phase Matrix

Phase	Concept	Design	Validation	Production
Purpose of Phase	*Exploring possibilities to meet customer needs*	*Complete detailed product design*	*Design & Process Validation Testing*	*Satisfy customer demand*
Product Marketing	• Market Requirements Document • Needs and Tasks Analyses • Initial Market Research	• Forecast Assumptions • Product Marketing Plan • Usability Reports	• Usability Validation Report • External Benchmarks • Initial Product Introduction Plans	• Price Plan • Product Launch Plans • Establish Listening Posts
Project Management	• Assign Project Leader • Create Preliminary Project Plan • Create Function Phase Matrix	• Manage Boundary Conditions • Manage Project Communications • Out of Bounds Review, if required	• Manage Boundary Conditions • Manage Project Communications • Ensure Test Coverage	• Manage Boundary Conditions • Manage Project Communications • Run Overall Post-Mortem
Software Engineering	• Create Preliminary S/W Project Plan • Create Preliminary Architecture • Create Preliminary Test Plan	• S/W Design Specification Completed • Test Plan & Schedule • Formal System Level Quality Review	• Final Candidate Software Release • Final Code Review • Software Accepted as GM Quality	• Software Project Plan Post-Mortem • GM Accpetance Testing • Final Test Report
Operations	• Preliminary Manufacturing Plan • Long Lead Components • Sole Source List	• Design For Manufacturability (DFM) Input • Supplier Management Strategy • Establish Global Ramp Plan	• Production Process Validated • Production Rev Test HW and SW Available • Standard Costs Established	• Outgoing Reliability & Quality Goals Achieved • Achieve Time to Efficiency Goals • Begin Field Failure Feedback

Function (row axis label)

Phase transition labels: Concept/Review · Design Maturity Review · Ready to Launch Review · Post-Mortem Review

What's New?

Companies launch new projects every day. Most of them get off to a fast start, but many of them do not get off to a good start. Projects can quickly get derailed when teams don't have a clear understanding of what each team member is contributing during each phase of the project. So how do you quickly construct and communicate milestone objectives and team-member contributions that highlight gaps and overlaps? The Function Phase Matrix is a powerful tool that will help you do just that.

Benefits

- Ensures that you have **cross-functional alignment** at the phase/milestone level
- Ensures you have **all key deliverables assigned** to individuals
- Is a **scalable tool** you can apply to large or small teams, simple or complex projects, and local or globally dispersed teams
- Helps you **align your team** with product and delivery expectations when you use it in management reviews

Which Business Problems Does the Tool Solve?

Many times, projects experience avoidable setbacks. The Function Phase Matrix can increase the effectiveness of a project team by clarifying roles and responsibilities early in the life of a project. It is one of the easiest ways to create a consistent development process. Additionally, a well-defined Function Phase Matrix helps accelerate the ramp up of new hires.

What Else Should You Know?

There are a few things to consider when applying this best practice. First, the tool doesn't include all functions and deliverables. Second, companies should consider the matrix as the start of process definition. Ultimately, the organization must define the roles/responsibilities of team members and the specifics of the deliverables (templates and examples).

Case Study

CleanCo is at the beginning phase of defining their first product delivery. The executive team (the CEO and product visionary, Wendy, the CTO and co-founder, Peter, and the multipurpose marketing manager, Bill) has decided that it is important to construct a Function Phase Matrix to clarify the key deliverables for the software teams. This is the first time the executive team has delegated product development to their expanding organization. To ensure that the new hires have a clear understanding of what elements they will deliver throughout the development lifecycle, the project manager, Bill, has constructed a Function Phase Matrix to identify and assign all the deliverables.

The executive team has reviewed and approved this general diagram and then handed it off to the project manager leading the product development. In one of their first cross-functional meetings, the team has reviewed and revised the template above to modify the deliverables as appropriate to this particular project and identify gaps and overlaps.

Setting Project Boundary Conditions

Boundary Conditions Diagram

What Is the Tool?

The Boundary Conditions Diagram is a tool that identifies the critical elements of a project and defines the conditions by which these elements must exist in order for a team to ship a successful product to market. When you apply it early in the development process, typically at the time of project funding, the Boundary Conditions Diagram creates a lightweight plan of record and helps keep your team focused on the most important aspects of the project. The Boundary Conditions Diagram identifies the three to four critical elements of a project (typically features, cost, schedule, and/or quality). You graphically represent the diagram as a triangle or square and assign each element to a side of the chosen object shape. You state the boundary for each element with specific conditions attached. Examples include:

- Product Cost: $X/unit, not to exceed Y% over the threshold

- Performance: X% increase over current product performance, but not <Y%

- Features: A, B, & C are "must-have" features. The product won't be viable without them

- Schedule: The product must be available for purchase by November 1, 2012

By implementing the Boundary Conditions Diagram early in the product development process, you create a "contract" between the project and management teams. This contract allows the team the authority to plan and execute the project with minimal intervention unless they cross the boundaries. Knowing that most projects run into challenges along the development path, we have also created a complimentary process, the Out-of-Bounds Check. When the team crosses the boundary conditions, they are required to execute the Out-of-Bounds Check, which helps to quickly get the team on track using the Boundary Conditions Diagram framework.

Defining project boundary conditions is an effective methodology that will drive subsequent project tradeoff decisions throughout the entire development process.

Visualization

The boundaries are shown on the edges of the triangular drawing. This drawing is presented throughout the process in meetings between management and the team. The Boundary Condition Diagram indicates the number of key boundary areas (in this case three, so it is a triangle), the name of each boundary in gray, and then the specific details defining the thresholds are described in the boxes next to each boundary.

WebCo Project Boundary Conditions

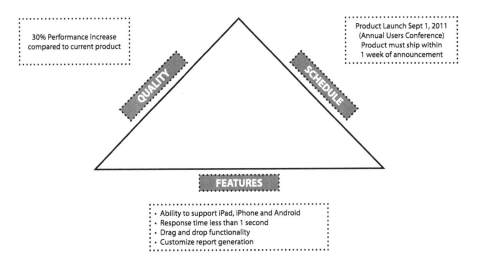

30% Performance increase compared to current product

Product Launch Sept 1, 2011 (Annual Users Conference) Product must ship within 1 week of announcement

QUALITY

SCHEDULE

FEATURES

- Ability to support iPad, iPhone and Android
- Response time less than 1 second
- Drag and drop functionality
- Customize report generation

What's New?

Executives are delegating more and more authority to teams. In order to give teams the authority they would like, the Out-of-Bounds Check provides a very clear representation of the key dimensions of a project. If the team is within bounds, executives do not need to micromanage. So this is a very clean way to pass control to teams without abdicating all responsibility. It is a win-win for contemporary product development teams and their managers.

Benefits

- **Accelerates innovation** by ensuring alignment and focus on the critical elements that define a successful project.

- Provides a clear **distinction of "must-have"** elements from the rest of the project scope.

- Creates a contract between your management and project teams to **allow more autonomy** for the team to plan and execute the project.

- Ensures you **make project trade-off decisions** in the context of boundary conditions, which will eliminate surprises later in the process.

- Provides for you a framework to **quickly realign** if the team crosses the boundary conditions.

Which Business Problems Does the Tool Solve?

Your best chance of delivering the right product at the right time is to ensure that project teams clearly understand the most important elements of a project. When you apply it early in the process, the Boundary Conditions Diagram ensures that you gain clarity and agreement on these elements and provides a clear framework for subsequent decision making. When you apply it throughout the process, it reduces the number of delays since top management does not have to constantly intervene.

What Else Should You Know?

Defining the small handful of boundaries and the levels for triggering a boundary break is not trivial. It is typically proposed by the team and approved by management at the first management check-in of the project. The Boundary Conditions Diagram is not a replacement for other project management tools. It complements tools and processes such as schedules, work breakdown structures, and project team meetings.

Case Study

A cross-functional product team is completing the concept phase of WebCo's next new product. A deliverable for this phase is a management check-in to present the progress and to obtain funding to move forward with the project. Included in the check-in is the Boundary Conditions Diagram, which contains the features, delivery schedule, and product performance that are required for WebCo to leapfrog the competition.

How to Quickly Get Projects Back on Track
Out-of-Bounds Check

What Is the Tool?

The Out-of-Bounds (OOB) Check is a process you can use to realign teams after a project has gone out of scope. It is a powerful process that provides the team with a mechanism to quickly conduct a root cause analysis, evaluate alternatives, and recommend a remedy to the project decision makers. Setting boundary conditions, which reflect the critical elements of a project (typically cost, schedule, features, and/or quality), at the time of project approval creates a "contract" between management and project teams. This contract allows teams to move forward with minimal guidance as long as they do not cross the boundary conditions. And when they cross those boundaries, the OOB Check is the mechanism to course correct and realign to a new plan of record.

When a project team detects (or anticipates at a high confidence level) that an OOB condition will occur, the program manager gathers relative information to determine if the team can resolve the issue and still maintain the boundary condition. If the team cannot, the program manager would craft an OOB communication and send it to key decision makers outlining:

1. Which project boundary the team will break/has broken

2. The root cause for the broken boundary

3. Alternatives to resolve the issue (with supporting schedule and/or cost-impact data)

4. The recommendation of the project team

The program manager can deliver this communication either via email or in a scheduled meeting. Key decision makers respond with either approval or a modified approach. To accelerate realignment, it is best to empower teams to communicate the recommendation and move forward unless they receive contrary directions.

It should be the intent of both the project team and key decision makers to complete this process quickly (within hours/days, not days/weeks).

Visualization

The Out-of-Bounds Check is a flow diagram where time flows from top to bottom, and the steps are shown in gray. The details of the gray boxes are shown to the right, and the diamond is a decision point. This diagram shows how easy it can be to perform the Out-of-Bounds check.

The Out-of-Bounds (OOB) Check

A face-to-face meeting with key decision makers is not practical due to international travel schedules, so the program manager provides the above information in an email to the decision makers and copies the core project team to accelerate the process. Management finally approves the two recommended solutions sent by email.

What's New?

What's new is a lean, fast, and effective process for aligning teams and management and getting them back on track when a project undergoes material changes that affect the plan of record. An organization's ability to respond quickly and effectively to any change is a fundamental characteristic that separates the marginal from the successful. Organizations can accomplish this by allowing teams to interact with management in a way based on trust that helps management be part of the solution, not part of the problem.

Rarely does a project go from start to completion without changes occurring along the way – both anticipated and unanticipated. Even with the best efforts to anticipate and mitigate project risks, sometimes projects go off the rails. And when this happens, more times than not it's difficult to refocus the team and get them back on track. There is often ambiguity around who makes the decisions that reset the course of the team and when those decisions are made. The benefit of this process is the complete clarity on what to do when a boundary break occurs.

Benefits

- Helps you **realign projects within hours/days**, not days/weeks.
- **Empowers the team** to move forward with minimal guidance once management establishes boundary conditions.
- **Minimizes confusion** within the team by establishing a single, agreed-upon communication vehicle.
- Engages the team because of the **greater trust** that management places in them.

Which Business Problems Does the Tool Solve?

This lightweight process is an effective recovery vehicle for when projects run into trouble. It creates a common language and mechanism to quickly align the project and management teams when a project changes significantly. There is no time wasted by each team trying to create an exception-handling process each time a deviation occurs. The result is faster decision making.

What Else Should You Know?

When getting started with the Out-of-Bounds Check process, it is important not to blame the program manager or react negatively to hearing bad news. In order to encourage open communication, management must welcome out-of-bounds communications and work with the team to get them back on track. If the organization is unsupportive of this new way of communicating bad news, the new process will not take root.

Case Study

A cross-functional product team is in the development phase of delivering WebCo's next new product. They have established the following boundary conditions for the project at the time of project approval and funding.

Project Boundary Conditions

Performance to equal
or
exceed previous release

Product Launch Sept 1, 2011
(Annual Users Conference)

QUALITY

SCHEDULE

FEATURES

- Ability to support iPad, iPhone and Android
- Response time less than 1 second
- Drag and drop functionality
- Customize report generation

The team, in the development phase, has begun delivering early builds to the quality team. Testing has uncovered a critical bug involving a third-party component. In order to debug and resolve the issue, the team needs the help of the third-party developers. However, this is a lower-priority problem for them, and they will not commit to a timetable for resolution. Product marketing does not want to ship the product without this functionality. The project manager and development lead determine that, if there is no resolution within two weeks, the project will break either the Feature Boundary or the Schedule Boundary. The project manager begins working with the development lead and product manager to analyze the root causes of this problem and evaluate alternatives to realign the boundary conditions.

Out-of-Bounds Process

1. **Description of broken boundary and impact on project**

   The team has discovered a critical bug in a third-party module. This module delivers a "must-have" feature for the release, which is scheduled to coincide with the annual industry conference. The bug is reproducible in approximately 25% of the test scenarios. However, this issue is not a high enough priority for the third-party developers, and they have not assigned resources to analyze or resolve it. The current impact is a delay in the schedule for four to six weeks.

2. **Alternatives**

   a. Form a tiger team to replicate the functionality and/or create a workaround for bug scenarios.
   b. Decouple the feature and continue developing while working on the issue in parallel.
   c. Continue with the current version of the module and fix the issue in the next release.
   d. Request executive intervention with the third-party management team to raise priority.

3. **Recommendation**

   a. Decouple the feature and continue developing while working on the issue in parallel.
   b. Request executive intervention with the third-party management team to raise priority.

Prioritizing Defects Through the Customer's Eyes

Bug Management Matrix

What Is the Tool?

The Bug Management Matrix contains a list of defects along with their descriptions, impact, and priority. The use of priority to focus on fixing defects is the most important aspect of this fresh outlook. The difference between this model and a more conventional bug analysis system is twofold: (1) the elimination of a bug severity rating; and (2) the increased focus on customer impact.

A bug that causes the a program to immediately crash is often referred to as a "blocker" — indicating that the existence of this bug would block you from shipping the product. Typically, blocker bugs would be assigned both the highest severity and priority ratings because of their large negative impact on the user. However, the two measures are redundant and create an unnecessary level of complexity. A measure better than severity is priority - the impact the bug will have on the customer and the frequency of the impact.

The above describes the most important column of the Bug Management Matrix. The remaining columns have to do with the customer experience (except for precedent), including the experience description from the user point of view, the impact on the user, the frequency of impact, and the impact on the support organization.

Organizations can use the Bug Management Matrix as the primary tool in bug-scrub meetings after they complete a QA testing run and there is a cross-functional review of the results. QA, program management, product management, engineering, and sometimes customer service attend the meeting. The new best practice is that product management runs the meeting and makes the final calls on the priority of the defect. Engineering and QA have inputs on how they will fix and verify the bug and may have some influence on its priority, but ultimately it is the product management's call. Based on priorities, limitations of staffing, and the difficulty of solution, product management may shift the priority of the defect to maximize the team's effectiveness.

Visualization

The visualization below shows an example of how organizations use this tool to prioritize bugs during bug-scrubbing sessions. The bug name is a hyperlink that points to the bug database, and the user priority definitions fall under the guidelines defined below. Both the issue summary and the description of the impact are from the user's perspective. The frequency of impact is an estimate of how frequently the issue could occur based on extrapolation from test results. The precedent provides background on similar defects. Finally, the support impact column indicates the estimated consequences of the defect on the support organization (or other support tools). The approach used with this matrix is more beneficial than most methods of bug-scrubbing in that it emphasises the customer's point of view throughout the remediation process.

Bug Management Matrix

Bug	User Priority	Issue Summary	User Impact / User Experience Description	Frequency of Impact	Precedent	Support Impact
PRO_S1-136	P1	Intermittently crashes when starting to record audio, just after performing save	Very negative and potential loss of data	10%	New Bug	Huge if released, as this will cause a support call
PRO_S1-108	P1	Audio recording has excess hiss during first 4 seconds	Many or all power users will detect this	100%	PRO_SO-512	Limited to power users, but they will complain in forums
PRO_S1-118	P2	Clicking and popping when pressing volume up or down button	This will be audible to all users, but the volume level of the pop noise is low	100%	PRO_SO-335	Limited
PRO_S1-217	P2	Installation process requires the USB cord be disconnected for Windows Vista	This bug does not occurr on Windows 7, but will on all Windows machines before Windows 7	40%	New Bug	Some installation support calls expected
PRO_S1-347	P3	Swishing of background noise when loud sound stops (compressor recovery)	Power audio users will notice, but may not complain	5%	New Bug	Limited or no impact
PRO_S1-318	P3	Pop noise detected when speaker is close to microphone	This will sometimes be a problem in the field, but users mostly understand you need to use a pop screen	25%	New Bug	Put on FAQ page, limited support calls expected

Below are some recommended user priority definitions for software defects:

- **P1:** Has a critical impact on user experience or brand and will block the release (examples include frequent program crashes, loss of data, or frozen screen).

- **P2:** Has a high impact on user experience or brand and will block the release (examples include loss of feature (no workaround), a rare program crash, or loss of data).

- **P3:** Has a medium impact on user experience or brand, and you should fix it before the release (examples include loss of feature (with workaround)).

- **P4:** Has a limited impact on user experience or brand, and you should fix it if time permits (examples include cosmetic minor color variation).

What's New?

The use of both severity and priority is confusing. Software development teams need to approach defect management with some fresh thinking, where the customer's perspective is the most important, and avoid internal parameters such as severity. The perspective of the customer, instead of QA or engineering, needs to drive the defect management process.

Benefits

- You create **better products** because the focus is on user experience.
- There is **less politics** because the matrix clearly specifies the roles of decision makers.
- You have more **efficient use of resources** because the team is ultimately focused on what matters.

Which Business Problems Does the Tool Solve?

There are business benefits in focusing the organization on making great products and efficiency benefits in ensuring that you have an effective bug-scrubbing process. First and foremost, all the benefits are for the customer because the matrix helps you see defects from the customer's perspective and their elimination aims to improve the customer experience.

In a software organization, much of the time consumed during development is in the late development and early testing phase extending to release. Any processes that can prioritize the work and focus the team on key tasks will directly improve efficiency. The same goes for any process that clarifies roles and speeds decision making. Here the effect is magnified due to the repetitive nature of this bug-scrubbing cycle. Having a clear focus on the user, coupled with an efficient decision-making process, will yield faster time-to-market and better products.

What Else Should You Know?

Product management must be a good proxy for the customer, so it is important for product managers to not insert their personal opinions into the process, but rather rely on a clear-eyed view of the customer's reaction. Engineering and QA must not bias their estimates of how long it will take to fix a bug, which can shift the priorities.

Case Study

WebCo, the software organization, was challenged with an ever-increasing debugging cycle time and changing priorities for debugging. The QA manager was very headstrong, viewed herself as the guardian of quality, and believed any steps to shorten validation time and reduce coverage would result in difficult field situations and a damaged reputation. Engineering was also very opinionated regarding which defects were important and which they should not work on. Since they knew what was under the hood, they felt they had the right perspective.

The CEO, Rajiv, was tired of the constant delays in the software release and felt that the whole process was not under control. What was most troubling was the fact that the schedule would slip week after week as the team would reclassify bugs and move them up in importance after the find/fix/verify cycle. After thinking about the perspectives of the various players in this process, Rajiv realized that the customer's perspective was the one that mattered.

Consequently, the organization simplified the process so that they would no longer use the severity rating and would give product management the ultimate responsibility for setting bug priority. The change in the organization was not immediate as the president had to remind engineering and QA of Molly's (product management) new role. However, the results were immediate in that the find/fix/verify cycle went from an average of ten working days down to seven, and the verification phase went down from 19 weeks to just over 14 weeks.

Execution

Merriam-Webster defines execution as "the act or mode or result of performance[1]." By definition, companies are "executing" every day to a plan (whether it's formal or informal and written or verbal). We frequently see product development teams very busy doing just that. But there always seems to be too much to do in too little time, and there is a lot of motion and little progress. We're not talking about execution as just the act of "doing" as quickly as possible. This section is about operational excellence – doing the right things at the right time in the most efficient manner to ensure your team delivers the right product at the right time.

Mark Zuckerberg has created five core values to describe how he runs Facebook. He included these in his S1 filing to the Securities and Exchange Commission. Four of these five values solidly express the core elements of execution:

1. Focus on Impact
2. Move Fast
3. Be Bold
4. Be Open
5. Build Social Value

Facebook's initial public offering is thought to be the largest IPO ever, and this is due in part to their excellence in execution.

Why Is This Section Important in Supporting Innovation and Time-to-Market?

If your goal is to increase innovation while reducing time-to-market, the key to achieving operational excellence through execution is to ensure that your teams are poised for success. It's critical that they have the best tools to create and optimize schedules, work efficiently, monitor and measure their progress, and then implement improvements (when required) as quickly as possible. Managers who overburden their teams, don't manage with predictive metrics, and don't prioritize work create a drag on their teams.

Sloppy execution increases the risk of hitting the cycle time goal (let alone shortening the cycle time) and distracts technical thought leaders from creating new and better ways to design products. Many times, one or more of these conditions result in a longer time-to-market and a marginalized product offering. And, of course, one of the worst outcomes of sloppy execution is delivering a poor product to your customers.

Use Cases Where You Apply These Tools

The graphical tools in this section provide you with your best chance of achieving operational excellence. They are a collection of best practices to optimize how your team executes. The first three chapters help you develop accurate schedules using the knowledge of your team and their past performance in delivering products to market. The next three chapters provide you with a clear-eyed view on the true health of a project. By implementing early warnings when something bad is about to happen and tracking your team's true progress, you have the data to make better decisions faster. The final two chapters provide tools to help you optimize the efficiency of your team and capture data about how your customers use your products and which features are most valuable to them.

Chapter & Tool Listing

Title	Tool
Reducing Schedule Through Teamwork	Team PERT Chart
Quickly Estimating Accurate Project Schedules	Lite Schedule Estimating Matrix
Precisely Estimating Accurate Project Schedules	Precise Schedule Estimating Matrix
Early Indicator of Schedule Risk	Schedule Prediction Accuracy Chart
Tracking Real-Time Progress	Task Burn Down Chart
Managing the Speed of Deliverables	Deliverable Hit Rate Chart
Optimizing Workloads Within a Function	Project Efficiency Chart
Using Communities to Understand Customer Usage	Community Product Requirements Chart

Reducing Schedule Through Teamwork
Team PERT Chart

What Is the Tool?

The Team PERT Chart is a group process to generate a schedule and help reduce time-to-market. PERT stands for **Program Evaluation** and **Review Technique** and is also known as CPM or Critical Path Method. This scheduling method has the benefit of showing the critical path (the sequence of events that describes the minimum time needed to complete a project), which is useful to project managers because reducing the time of tasks on the critical path will shorten the overall schedule. By using a team-based method to form this schedule, you will get a cross-functional buy-in and end up with a schedule your team can support.

Your team creates the schedule in real time in a workshop setting, using notecards to represent the tasks. The session starts with a description of the project and a request for each member to write down tasks they see as important to the project. They arrange the tasks in a network diagram from left to right without the use of any technology. If any milestones are more than two weeks apart, the team needs to break down the tasks so that the longest interval is two weeks. Your team then draws arrows on notecards between the tasks and lists the range of times needed to complete a given task below its name in the notecard.

After they complete the diagram, they determine the critical path. Then the team works collaboratively to figure out how they can reduce the critical path by discussing tricks to shorten the longest times on the critical path. Once the team has minimized the schedule, they can import this new information into the software you use to manage projects. It is also easy to convert the PERT diagram into a Gantt chart showing the project milestones and the timelines to achieve them. Gantt charts are best for tracking schedules because they are easy to update, while PERT charts are best for creating schedules because they reveal dependent tasks and focus the team on shortening the critical path.

You typically estimate the duration of each task by creating three estimates for the time - the optimistic (O = shortest), the pessimistic (P = longest), and the typical (T = average). You combine these to generate the estimated task duration using the formula $(O + 4*T + P)/6$. Research by the U.S. Navy has led to this method, which helps provide a way to quickly estimate the most likely duration of each task since determining ranges is always easier than picking a single number.

Visualization

This visualization of the project shows the beginning stage, between the Market Requirements Document (MRD) and the Concept Check-in, where management approves the project. The critical path appears in the larger gray dotted line, and the numbers at the bottom are the times needed to complete the tasks (in weeks). The first number is the optimistic estimate, the middle number is the typical duration, and the last number is the pessimistic estimate. The estimated time is a weighted average of the three times.

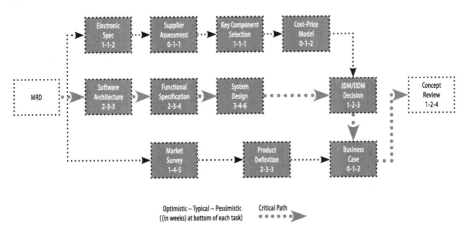

Optimistic – Typical – Pessimistic   Critical Path
((in weeks) at bottom of each task)

The table below shows the calculated times for each task and the duration of this stage based on summing the times in the critical path. Only the time between the MRD and the Concept Check-in is shown. The remainder of the project took an additional 45 weeks, so the total duration of the project is 60 weeks.

Task	Optimistic	Typical	Pessimistic	Average	Critical Path
MRD					
Electronic Spec	1	1	2	1.2	
Supplier Assessment	0	1	1	0.8	
Key Component Selection	1	1	1	1.0	
Cost-Price Model	0	1	2	1.0	
JDM/ODM Decision	1	2	3	2.0	2.0
Software Architecture	2	3	3	2.8	2.8
Functional Specification	2	3	4	3.0	3.0
System Design	3	4	6	4.2	4.2
Market Survey	1	4	5	3.7	
Product Definition	2	3	3	2.8	
Business Case	0	1	2	1.0	1.0
Concept Check-in	1	2	4	2.2	2.2
Total Weeks					15.2

What's New?

The Team PERT Chart provides a way to empower teams to create their own schedule because the management trend is to delegate more authority to the team. It promotes a "bottom-up" management approach rather than the old-fashioned "top-down" way of command and control.

The Team PERT Chart supports the trend toward more collaborative team involvement since the project manager does not dominate the scheduling process. Managers are often the facilitators of the group process, but they do not force dates and deliverables on team members. In this newer collaborative setting, the PERT process also gives all functions an equal voice to describe the key milestones they need to achieve.

Benefits

- Focuses on the critical path to **reduce the overall cycle time**
- Is a **fast method** to create schedules
- Ensures **cross-functional alignment and buy-in** to the tasks and timeline
- Provides accurate estimates of the **time needed to complete each task**
- **Eliminates the need for complex and expensive** project management software

Which Business Problems Does the Tool Solve?

The Team PERT Chart reduces time-to-market because it forces the team to understand what is really on the critical path and helps them reduce its duration. The chart can also reduce time-to-market because it encourages parallelism through giving the various functions on the team (marketing, sales, operations, engineering, quality, customer service, and legal) flexibility to sequence activities off the critical path and do more in parallel.

The Team PERT Chart increases predictability because it gets all the functional inputs into key milestones to ensure that your team does not inadvertently omit key tasks. Furthermore, because your team creates the schedule themselves, they will strive to support it. This team process increases predictability because the group comes up with small tasks that are no more than two weeks apart. This forces really hard thinking about the project details.

What Else Should You Know?

In order to generate a quality schedule, your team needs to dedicate the time necessary to work through the process. The hard thinking that goes into the process comes from the requirement that tasks be small. The Team PERT Chart works best if you have the entire cross-functional team present for the work session. The accuracy of the schedule depends on the experience of the team creating it, so it is important to ensure as much as possible that there are experienced team members in the room. If there are some gaps in experience, it is possible to supplement your team with outside members who can help in the scheduling process.

Case Study

NetCo was planning their next product launch for a business-critical offering. The EVP of engineering (Bill) demanded that the launch be in four quarters. Richard, the project manager who ran the PMO, pushed back on Bill and said he couldn't predict the schedule of a project that did not have a defined set of requirements. Fortunately, Bill agreed and asked the head of marketing to put her best product manager on the project and develop a Market Requirements Document (MRD). Once Richard had the MRD in hand, he created an offsite to generate a team-based PERT schedule.

Day One (Afternoon Only)

The team reviewed the MRD and clarified some key open issues with the product manager, who was part of the offsite. Once Richard had a clear target, he presented the team with a similar completed project so that they knew what a typical effort looked like. Then the team worked on creating a half-dozen high-level milestones based on the product development process at NetCo. The team members individually wrote down key tasks to get from one major milestone to the next. They also wrote down on the notecards the optimistic, typical, and pessimistic estimates for the duration (in days) of each task.

Day Two (All Day)

Richard reconvened the team and asked them one by one to put their notecards on the white board and group together any redundant cards they came across. The team worked on putting arrows between the various tasks to create the network diagram and linked the tasks with dependent prior tasks. This was a good time for the team to do an omissions check to see if they omitted any key tasks and do a sanity check on some of the durations that looked out of line (they created the durations using the formula $(O + 4*T + P)/6$). Given this clean draft, the team determined the critical path and highlighted it on the white board by making it darker than the other arrows connecting the tasks. For simplicity, the diagram shown earlier in the chapter only displays the project from MRD to the Concept Check-in, which is only 15 out of the total 60 week program.

During the afternoon, the team broke into several small groups to brainstorm how to shorten the critical path. They discussed a number of solutions and, based on consensus, integrated them into the diagram. This process took approximately 12 weeks off of a 60-week schedule, resulting in an aggressive 48-week schedule with a critical path so optimized that, if the team shortened it any more, the schedule would run against several paths that were difficult to shrink. The team was satisfied with their work product and took a picture of the notecards on the wall so they could import them into presentation software. Richard took action to create a Gantt chart.

The result was a highly optimized and detailed schedule with a team buy-in that Bill and the rest of the executives accepted as the best shot at the shortest time-to-market. Bill was also delighted that the schedule was shorter than the 52-week goal he put forward to the team at the beginning of the project.

Quickly Estimating Accurate Project Schedules

Lite Schedule Estimating Matrix

Wayne Mackey

What Is the Tool?

The Lite Schedule Estimating Matrix is a parametric tool that guides the estimation of the amount of time a project takes in a given phase by using experience combined with the "critical few" key drivers that impact schedule. The matrix, which consists of five to eight inputs per phase, will predict the duration of each phase based on the range of typical times and the technical complexity of the design.

The purpose of the Lite Schedule Estimating Matrix is twofold. The first is to help inexperienced program managers be more successful, and the second is to help communicate the schedule duration to management. The tool also provides an alternative to the time-consuming bottom-up Gantt chart (although we recommend that you use both in most situations).

You construct this spreadsheet-based tool by vertically inputting phases down the rows, with the time estimates and complexity inputs represented horizontally across the columns for each phase. In the first column are the critical few schedule drivers that come from your organization. You can tap the knowledge of the organization by collecting the drivers from the most experienced project managers in the organization. Examples of these drivers for a software project might be the number of screens/pages, number of interfaces, complexity of system integration, percentage of testing that is automated, and number of geographies. The second and third columns are the historical range of these drivers (in number or in percentage) represented as low to high. The fourth column is your estimate of the complexity of the project, and the fifth column is open for comments. The matrix also indicates the historical range of months for each phase. After entering all the estimates for the drivers in a phase, the project manager applies judgment to indicate what the duration of the phase would be, given the various answers to the individual drivers.

The program manager can use this tool alone; however, the results will be more accurate if the cross-functional team works together to come up with the estimates. In the case of very complex systems, it is possible to decompose the estimation into software, hardware, accessories, etc. After coming up with the individual estimates, the program managers for the subsections should provide an integrated estimate, taking advantage of parallelism that is available in most programs.

Visualization

Lite Schedule Estimating Matrix

Team			Enter project name	
Phases and Drivers	**Historical**	**range**	**Estimate**	**Data, comments or explanation**
1. Concept	1	6	**(Enter # months)**	
Key Drivers				
New to Company (75%)/New to World (100%)	10%	100%	Enter # processes	
Number of new architectural blocks	4	6	Enter # new interfaces	
Number of major new technologies required	1	2	Enter # technologies	
Relative access vs. need for specific deep technical experience	0%	100%	Enter % of access	
Available resources planned vs. available	20%	100%	Enter % of optimum	
2. Design	1	14	**(Enter # months)**	
Key Drivers				
Percentage of interfaces fully defined	0%	100%	Enter % defined	
Relative complexity of system integration	0	20	Enter # new integrations	
Percentage of design reuse	0%	100%	Enter % reuse	
Number of new subcomponent vendors	0	7	Enter # new vendors	
Relative access vs. need for specific deep technical experience	0%	100%	Enter % of access	
Available resources planned vs. available	20%	100%	Enter % of optimum	
3. Development	1	10	**(Enter # months)**	
Key Drivers				
Percentage of the specification with quantified test limits	20%	100%	Enter % of spec	
Number of subsystems to be verified	1	20	Enter # subsystems	
Percentage of automated testing that will be in place at the end of development	10%	100%	Enter % of code covered	
Number of iterations – due to spec rigor and/or coupled designs feature creep	1	7	Enter # iterations	
Available resources planned vs. available	20%	100%	Enter % of optimum	
4. Validation	1	4	**(Enter # months)**	
Key Drivers				
Enter complexity of hardware/software combination	0%	100%	Enter % new HW involved	
Number of geographic targeted	1	4	Enter # geographies	
Safety & Regulatory clearance in above geographies?	1	4	Enter # geographies	
Predictability of the rate of cases for validation	0%	100%	Enter % of predicted cases	

The above visualization shows the blank table template. You need to modify it for your drivers and projects. It can be helpful in many cases to have different estimation charts for hardware, software, accessories, etc. The key drivers detail out different components that drive schedule, the historical range shows the range of data in previous programs, and the estimate column allows space for the entry of your estimate of this project under evaluation. The last row of each phase allows you to enter a duration based on your subjective impression of relative complexity of the various drivers.

What's New?

There is more rapid development going on now than there was at any point in history. For example, Web 2.0 development and smart phone applications can have releases every week! With this very fast release cycle, there is a great opportunity to improve schedule estimation because the cycles of learning are so short. Quick improvement is possible.

In general, organizations need to adapt and move more quickly, as the world is a lot less forgiving when it comes to being late. Beyond just late schedule, extended enterprise design and development require synchronization of disparate groups. With the rising standards in many areas (for example, overnight shipping or downloading apps instantly), predictability is now very important.

Benefits

- **Improves the predictability of schedules** since organizations can learn from past schedules
- **Reduces conflict** between the team and management
- As companies become more efficient **the value of the tool will grow over time**
- Is a **powerful method to capture institutional knowledge**, especially given the turnover
- **Establishes a common language** and one consistent visual tool for schedule estimation

Which Business Problems Does the Tool Solve?

Fundamentally, the Lite Schedule Estimating Matrix is a way to generate schedule estimates quickly.

What Else Should You Know?

There are several factors that can limit the accuracy of the method. The most important is that if the design paradigm changes, you may not have correct or sufficient baselines. For example, if you have just started to implement an agile software methodology, this means that the underlying process has dramatically changed and you will need to collect a new set of historical data from projects using the agile methodology. Another factor is that the estimation is inherently subjective, so the estimation quality is dependent on the skills of the team doing the estimate. However, in our experience, we found this tool to be almost twice as accurate as an average program manager, though less accurate than the best possible program manager. An alternative to this tool is the Precise Schedule Estimating Matrix, which provides a higher level of schedule accuracy, but requires greater effort to implement.

Case Study

One of the technology organizations within WebCo has about 100 contributors. They were having trouble with morale because, with their current efforts in getting new products to market, the schedule kept slipping. In January, the CEO asked the team to plan a follow up on their product line with a new release for the next selling season. The CEO gave the team the Market Requirements Document and asked if they could hit the deadline. In the past, it was simply a yelling match where engineering agreed to a deadline and then (unfortunately) did not hit it. This time around was going to be different.

Using the most experienced project manager and the engineer who started the company, the organization decided to put together a parametric Lite Schedule Estimating Matrix. They collected data over the last three years of releases dating back to the start of the company and determined the drivers (by phase) and then the range of dates from historical data. From this set of data, they had several additional project managers apply it to former projects. After doing this test on former projects, they ended up adding a driver that looks at resources available versus required, and they changed some of the historical data range. Then they applied the estimation process to the project they were planning. The result indicated that the project would miss the Fall by one quarter. Armed with this data and the Market Requirements Document, the project team was able to convince management to shed some features to ensure that the product would hit the timeline.

The result was even better than predicted. The team not only hit the deadline, but was also able to eliminate a schedule slip and avoid costly air freight.

Precisely Estimating Accurate Project Schedules

Precise Schedule Estimating Matrix

What Is the Tool?

Your past performance is the best predictor of future behavior, and in the absence of additional information, leveraging historical estimates is the best place to begin estimation. The Precise Schedule Estimating Matrix is a parametric tool that takes as an input a relative complexity rating (1-5) for key design blocks and produces as an output the estimated time-to-market and the person months required for key functions. The underlying algorithm is multivariate linear regression, and it is frequently used in statistics but not so often in product development.

Multivariable linear regression is a mathematical method that takes a set of data (input variables) and generates the best-fit output variables (the closest estimate based on experimental data), based on a set of coefficients that are derived by looking at many sample cases. In the simplest case, there have been estimates of software development time for iPhone™ applications that look like this:

$$\text{Time to release (in person days)} = 1\text{ day} + 0.6 * \text{number of screens}$$

So, for a three-screen application, we are estimating that the time-to-market would be on the order of three person days (2.8 actually). In this example, you can see that it is easy to estimate the number of days you need to develop an iPhone application. Obviously this is just an estimate, but it is much better than an estimate pulled without historical data.

Visualization

The visualization below shows an application of the Precise Schedule Estimating Matrix. The left-hand side consists of the input variables – the degree of complexity for hardware and software, the speed of the device, and the number of ports. The second to the last column is the output of the regression, predicting the person months required for hardware and software and the estimated time-to-market. The Range and Input columns represent typical complexity values and the corresponding entry of your assessmeent of this program. You need to modify this model for your drivers and projects.

Precise Schedule Estimating Matrix

Driver	Range	Input Estimates	Results	Units
HW Complexity	1 = cosmetic changes 3 = incremental with same silicon 5 = new silicon	3	35	Person Months
SW Complexity	1 = bug fixes only 3 = major feature enhancements 5 = new platform	3	87	Person Months
Speed	1 = 1G 3 = 10G 5 = 40G	1	22	Person Months
Ports	1 = 16 2 = 24 3 = 32 4 = 64 5 = 128	2	45	Person Months
Time-to-Market			16	Months

What's New?

The new aspects of this tool are similar to those of the Lite Schedule Estimating Matrix, but, because of the historical learning, there are some additional aspects that make this tool even timelier.

One of the more common ways to do agile development is to use user stories and ascribe points (called story points) to the use cases. If you collect historical data on the number of days a story point takes, you can use that data as an input to the linear regression.

You can use this tool to see the gain in productivity when offshoring to give you an objective and accurate reading of the benefits of your offshore efforts. This enables you to generate more accurate comparisons than those you have made in the past because you can normalize the comparisons between the complexity of two different projects given to two different organizations – onshore and offshore.

There are environmental and internal changes that make schedule estimation take on a new level of importance. Parametric schedule estimation takes advantage of this new realm by rapidly providing (in less than 15 minutes) schedule estimates based on historical data. These estimates can be more accurate than those created by a bottom-up Gantt chart and always engender a more rational discussion than that produced by ad-hoc "guestimates."

Benefits

- **Improves the predictability of schedules.** Organizations can learn from past schedules and apply good judgment.

- **Reduces conflict between the team and management** when it comes to schedule estimates

- Can start with basic information and gain accuracy over time. As you become more efficient in the methodology, **the value of the tool will grow over time**.

- Is a **powerful method to capture your institutional knowledge**, especially given the turnover in most organizations

- **Establishes a common language** and one consistent visual tool for schedule estimation

- Is **more accurate than other estimation tools** that do not apply linear regression

Which Business Problems Does the Tool Solve?

Like the Lite Schedule Estimating Matrix, this tool provides a way to generate schedule estimates quickly.

What Else Should You Know?

This method can be relatively accurate. It is more accurate than both an average program manager and a light parametric tool that does not rely on linear regression (see Lite Schedule Estimating Matrix). However, there is a price you must pay for this accuracy. Since this method relies on historical data, your organization must collect historical project data (time records and durations) in order to use it. Furthermore, you must have a significant number of projects in the database (on the order of 30, although it is possible to do it with fewer), and there must not be any significant changes in platforms or paradigms in the ensemble you use for deriving the estimates.

Case Study

One of the technology organizations within NetCo has about 200 contributors. They have instituted a schedule estimating model, the Lite Schedule Estimating Matrix, which is based on some rough estimates of complexity, but does not give them the kind of accuracy they now need in the current environment. The EVP of engineering, Bill, is interested in coming up with more accurate schedule estimates based on historical data. He also wants to see if his organization is improving its productivity over time. He would like to normalize projects by complexity and see if the number of person hours is going down since he has recently spent $5 M on computer-aided design (CAD) tools. He is expecting to see a measurable improvement in productivity and wants the analysis to incorporate the difference in complexity in various programs.

Bill asks Richard, the head of the program management office (PMO), to look into this and provide a model they can use in future schedules. Since the PMO tracks project expenses, from which they can get labor hours, it makes sense for Richard to run the project. Richard gets together a very small team to do the analysis, consisting of himself, a member of the research team who understands multivariate linear regression, and the CTO who knows what drives resources and time-to-market in their designs.

The CTO looks at their product families and starts dissecting the drivers. He determines that there are probably four drivers that might explain 80-90% of the effort in a product (network routing device sold to businesses). These include the complexity of the hardware design (whether it is new or a derivative of a prior model), the total number of ports in the device (16, 24, 32, 64, or 128), the speed of the device (1G, 10G, or 40G), and the difficulty of the embedded software (the degree of complexity of the software written on Linux 2.4).

For each of these complexity drivers, the CTO derives a scale that follows the guidelines below:

1. Hardware: 1 = cosmetic changes, 3 = incremental improvement with same silicon, and 5 = new silicon

2. Software: 1= bug fixes only, 3 = major feature enhancements, and 5 = new platform

3. Speed of device: 1 = 1G, 3 = 10G, and 5 = 40G

4. Number of ports: 1-5 = 16-128

In addition, the CTO provides examples for each driver so that project managers can use anchor points to improve the accuracy of their prediction (e.g., software that has a complexity rating of 3 would be typical of a product similar to ZP2000, ZP2002, ZQ2000, and ZQ2002 from NetCo's product line).

The goal is to estimate the number of software and hardware engineers and the overall time-to-market. The researcher takes the historical data and runs a four-variable regression with three output variables. They then test it on some of the 30 products that the research uses, and they find good accuracy (within 10% on resources and 15% on time-to-market).

NetCo has rolled out this model to the PMO. It is now part of the development process, and they also use it for budgeting and manpower planning. It is too early to see the success of the model, but so far it has provided Bill with a really good way to normalize his development productivity and offered product management a method to get better visibility into the estimated release date.

Early Indicator of Schedule Risk
Schedule Prediction Accuracy Chart

What Is the Tool?

The Schedule Prediction Accuracy Chart provides an early warning when a project fails to hit its expected schedule. This tool allows project teams to anticipate problems before they occur and to intervene before projects get behind schedule. The chart is a graphical representation of a series of schedules over time, highlighting how a project's major milestones are changing over time.

You construct the Schedule Prediction Accuracy Chart from an XY scatter plot, where the Y axis represents the predicted date when the project will achieve a milestone against the current prediction for the milestone (represented by the X axis). To gain the best accuracy, you should update the tool on a regular basis (typically weekly). Ideally, if a project experiences no schedule impacts, each milestone will appear over time as a horizontal line. When you introduce (or anticipate) schedule changes, the impact appears as an upward slope of the line. This tool also includes a "finish line", which is a diagonal line that represents when the project should reach each milestone based on the initial plan. By using a pre-populated template, it typically takes less than 15 minutes for the project manager to update the chart. The Schedule Prediction Accuracy Chart is more useful than the traditional Gantt chart because it (1) maintains the initial plan of record; (2) shows how a delay ripples through the schedule; (3) tracks the series of schedule estimates over time: and (4) visually displays the compression of future milestones.

Visualization

The Schedule Prediction Accuracy Chart below represents the schedule gaps between when the milestone was predicted to occur and the current prediction of the milestone. The vertical axis indicates when a milestone is predicted, and the horizontal axis indicates the date of the prediction. As seen below, the project experienced delays in three areas, which are labeled with the causes of the delays.

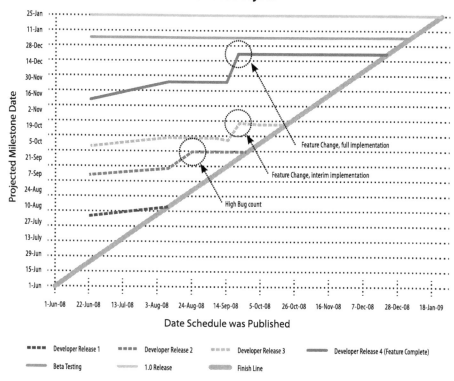

Schedule Prediction Accuracy Chart
CleanCo Project

Projected Milestone Date (y-axis): 25-Jan, 11-Jan, 28-Dec, 14-Dec, 30-Nov, 16-Nov, 2-Nov, 19-Oct, 5-Oct, 21-Sep, 7-Sep, 24-Aug, 10-Aug, 27-July, 13-July, 29-Jun, 15-Jun, 1-Jun

Date Schedule was Published (x-axis): 1-Jun-08, 22-Jun-08, 13-Jul-08, 3-Aug-08, 24-Aug-08, 14-Sep-08, 5-Oct-08, 26-Oct-08, 16-Nov-08, 7-Dec-08, 28-Dec-08, 18-Jan-09

Feature Change, full implementation
Feature Change, interim implementation
High Bug count

Legend: Developer Release 1, Developer Release 2, Developer Release 3, Developer Release 4 (Feature Complete), Beta Testing, 1.0 Release, Finish Line

What's New?

Avoidable delays in delivering products to market are fatal to companies, but we see them happen every day. Hoping that teams recover through their own heroic efforts only creates more chaos, not better results. The Schedule Prediction Accuracy Chart provides the best and earliest indication that a project is in jeopardy. Once project managers set up the Schedule Prediction Accuracy Chart with the key project milestones, it requires only a few minutes to update.

Benefits

- Serves as an **early warning sign** to prevent projects from going off track and gives the team the best chance of avoiding disasters.
- Is a tactically straightforward, but strategically powerful tool that drives **better decisions faster**.
- Provides a robust **visualization of the entire project over time**, with a visual emphasis on significant changes in schedule.
- Identifies back-end milestone compression to drive **risk reduction earlier into the process**.
- **Increases accountability** for the program manager
- **Eliminates the schedule gaming** that teams often go through by not including the original plan of record

Which Business Problems Does the Tool Solve?

Predicting problems before they occur is the greatest benefit of the Schedule Prediction Accuracy Chart.

The Schedule Prediction Accuracy Chart is an effective way to accelerate time-to-market by the early detection and elimination of project risks. Unlike other methods that graphically represent performance to schedule, this tool frames the current condition in the context of the original plan to provide a better insight into the true health of the project.

What Else Should You Know?

Initially, there is a learning curve to construct and interpret the tool. Most organizations have relied on the traditional Gantt chart and are familiar with managing to the current snapshot of a project. This tool requires a reframing of how you look at schedule performance to plan.

While this tool provides a clear assessment of the overall health of a project and the likelihood of achieving the project schedule goals, it doesn't address the root causes that drive schedule impacts. However, the successful implementation of this tool will provide the framework to conduct a well-focused root cause analysis.

Case Study

CleanCo was racing to deliver their first product to market. Time-to-market is critical for them to hit their revenue commitments for the fiscal year. They structured the product to include multiple development releases before the final 1.0 Release. The project manager switched from the traditional Gantt chart to the Schedule Prediction Accuracy Chart as a way of communicating the performance of the team, thus providing a better line of sight to the overall health of the project. The senior leadership team received project updates on a weekly basis or on an as-needed basis when escalations occurred. The visualization above illustrates the results of applying this tool.

After the rollout of Developer Release 2, product management re-evaluated the feature set for the 1.0 Release. They added new features to ensure the product was compelling and competitive. To protect the 1.0 Release schedule, they decided to split the implementation of the features across Developer Releases 3 and 4. Both releases experienced a schedule bump that allowed sufficient beta testing and the delivery of the 1.0 Release on time.

Tracking Real-Time Progress

Task Burn Down Chart

What Is the Tool?

The Task Burn Down Chart is an application of the agile development methodology. The essence of agile development is turning user stories into functioning code and testing them with a proxy for the customer in short iterations lasting two weeks or less. Each cycle is called a sprint, with the goal of doing as many use cases (or user stories) as possible in each sprint. As your team completes each sprint, they address a number of user stories and plan the next sprint to make further progress. At the end of each day, the customer representative on the team accepts a number of use cases and subtracts them from the total. This allows the team to see how rapidly they have burned down use cases during the sprint.

The team would list the number of use cases over a given sprint period, which indicates the number of use cases per week. This, along with the number of sprints, would yield the development duration. In order to estimate the length of a given development effort, the project manager would divide the number of user stories per sprint by the number of sprints and multiply the result by the duration of the sprints. However, things change. The team can knock off more (or fewer) user stories per sprint. The team can have the user stories change, so there are more (or less) to code. This tool allows the team to dynamically estimate the completion date based on the extrapolation of real project data.

With an understanding of agile development, the team can now frame out the role of the Task Burn Down Chart. It is a living bar chart that shows the team and management how much progress they are making on a project. The vertical axis is the number of user stories that the team puts into the release. The horizontal axis is the sprint number, which can be equivalent to a time scale. Because the number of use cases can change, it is possible to add a representation of the number of new user stories below the horizontal axis. The Task Burn Down Chart is much more meaningful than a Gantt chart since the graph includes on the vertical axis the number of user stories, which tells you how much actual work has been accomplished and is remaining in the project. Gantt charts only contain schedule information, not work information.

The team draws a target line from the starting point of the total number of use cases, extrapolating from the slope of the user stories over time. They extrapolate another target line from the number of user stories added below the horizontal axis, based on the trend of the number of additional user stories. Where these two lines intersect is the projected sprint number when the team finishes the project.

To gain the greatest benefit, the team should create a large poster of the Task Burn Down Chart and post it in their workspace.

Visualization

Below is an application of the Task Burn Down Chart. The vertical axis indicates the number of Story Points within a sprint, and the horizontal axis indicates the number of sprints. In this visualization, you can see that the IT department's implementation of the social media strategy does not go in a straight line, because new story points have been added at the third sprint. The IT department did this with management's knowledge and approval, resulting in a project that met or exceeded management's expectations because they added some needed use cases from HR late in the process that made this a much more user-friendly system.

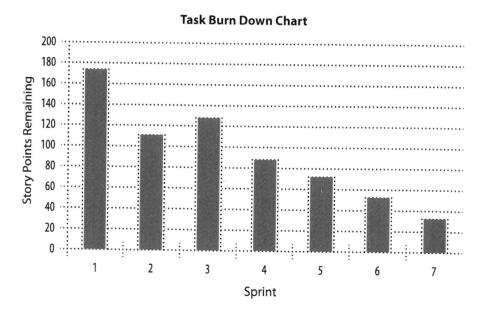

Task Burn Down Chart

What's New?

Software development has migrated to some degree from the waterfall model, where there is a clear handoff from one stage to the next, to agile development, where development is iterative. In agile development, the team goes through a whole development cycle (build/integrate/test cycle) many times, building up the number of use cases. Tracking the number of user stories completed per build is an emerging practice that combines many best practices in one easy-to-use system that allows management to actually see progress in software. It makes the invisible visible.

Benefits

- Focuses on the customer, as the primary vertical axis indicates the number of user stories and the team **makes trade-offs in the context of customer impact**.
- **Follows the best practice of predictive metrics**, so the team can course correct early in the process.
- Displayed in an **easy-to-understand graphical representation**, so team members can see where they are in the process and where they are headed.
- Shows the actual work that the team delivers, so it is a **true measure of progress**.

Which Business Problems Does the Tool Solve?

The most important benefit of this chart is that it keeps your project and management teams focused on what matters in product development - delivering features that are most important to customers in the fastest and most innovative way possible. The Task Burn Down Chart also supports innovation because it allows for the addition of new features during development.

What Else Should You Know?

There are many key factors to successful deployment, but the most important is to properly capture user stories in the first place. If you do not properly collect requirements, then you will go on a path that will not lead to the project's success.

Another risk factor is that user stories get watered down during execution so that you do not deliver the full functionality during the sprint. Having a strong customer representative in the process can help minimize this impact.

Finally, you need to place a fair amount of effort into updating this chart. You must place the responsibility for updating agile metrics onto one of your team members to ensure accurate and timely metrics.

Case Study

The IT department of WebCo was developing a social media strategy for corporate-wide implementation of a pilot rollout with a technology partner. They agreed on an agile development approach to the project and assigned members from both companies to the team. This team settled on two-week sprints and was anticipating eight of them to get the project done.

In the past, management used waterfall development, and, with multiple exceptions to the structured reviews approach, they never really knew where the project stood. However, in this case, the agile development method utilizing the Task Burn Down Chart proved instrumental from the beginning. For example, this process forced the business analyst to clearly identify most of the user stories at the beginning of the project. In the past, management did this in a sloppy fashion, and only in the pilot stage did they know that the requirements were incomplete.

Utilizing the Task Burn Down Chart to display progress, management could carry out the initial plan and see how, at the third sprint, the user stories took a jump up. This caused a management review half way through the pilot development and the resetting of management's expectations. The result was a better system delivery, with dates that management could accept because they were notified earlier.

Managing the Speed of Deliverables
Deliverable Hit Rate Chart

What Is the Tool?

The Deliverable Hit Rate Chart monitors the progress of completed tasks against a target over time. Best applied to complex programs with a large number of tasks, the tool is a high-level graphical representation that indicates whether the rate of task completion is on track for delivering the program on time.

You can construct the Deliverable Hit Rate Chart by dividing the total number of tasks required to complete the program by the duration of the program (typically measured in months). At the end of each month, you map the number of completed tasks against the target for that time period. You then update the line chart to present the actual deliverable hit rate.

Visualization

The visualization below describes the application of the Deliverable Hit Rate Chart. The vertical axis defines the total number of tasks that are tracked in the project, and the horizontal axis is a function of time (in this case measured in months) as defined by the project schedule. As seen in the visualization below, the team gets off to a good start, but then falls behind. The Deliverable Hit Rate Chart shows the contrast between the targeted and the actual rates of completed tasks. It can then be supplemented with specifics from the work breakdown structure to create a plan for getting back on track for a July delivery.

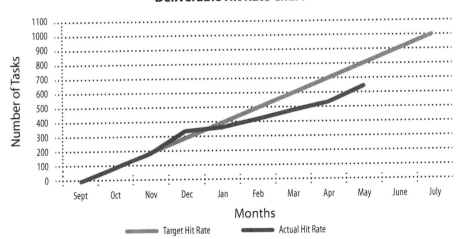

Deliverable Hit Rate Chart

What's New?

This chart allows a manager to step above all the details and get an accurate read on whether or not the team is moving at a speed that will result in an on-time delivery of the project. Like the Task Burn Down Chart, the Deliverable Hit Rate Chart shows actual work against plan.

Benefits

- ◉ The Deliverable Hit Rate Chart is a **high-level snapshot** that indicates whether or not a large program is on track for an on-time delivery.
- ◉ The tool is easy to construct and **provides an early warning when the team is not executing** to the target number of tasks, thus driving corrective action to get the team back on track.
- ◉ It is an **elegant solution for communicating a large amount of data** in an easy-to-interpret graphical representation.

Which Business Problems Does the Tool Solve?

The Deliverable Hit Rate Chart, like the Task Burn Down Chart, shows true work accomplished versus plan. It makes software development progress visible.

What Else Should You Know?

While it's an indicator of the speed of tasks you are accomplishing, this tool does not discern between the sizes of tasks. The quality of the output from this tool is dependent on tasks being relatively small, numerous, and roughly of the same size.

Case Study

NetCo is delivering a new product to market that requires contribution from 13 different teams. There are 60 people working on the project. Richard, the program manager, has constructed a large work breakdown structure that includes a low level of task granularity (no task has greater than a 40-hour level of effort), with milestones, interdependencies, and resources. In addition to managing the work breakdown structure, he needs to provide monthly management updates to demonstrate the progress of the team. To provide a high-level overview of the team's performance to plan, he constructs a Deliverable Hit Rate Chart. As you can see from the chart the team has been slipping since January and they are planning a design review in May to get the project back on track.

Optimizing Workloads Within a Function
Project Efficiency Chart

What Is the Tool?

The Project Efficiency Chart estimates the amount of time a project team has available to create useful work output based on the number of projects per person.

To apply the Project Efficiency Chart, tally up the number of initiatives each function (project engineering, user interaction design, and project management) is working on, counting every project, large or small. If there are tiny projects that take only 1-5% of their time, group them together as one "small collection" and assign them as one project that takes up to 10-20% of an individual's time. The typical result would be one to seven projects per person. Create a histogram, identifying the frequency of a given function with only one project, two projects, and so on, up to seven projects. Divide this by the total number of individuals in a function to get a percentage distribution.

You can then plug this histogram into the Project Efficiency Chart, which will predict the average value-added contribution of your organization across all functions. By looking at this result (usually shocking because of the low net productivity), your organization can re-examine its priority list and delay some of the current projects. Although this will reduce the number of projects they are currently working on, the actual throughput of the organization will be higher.

Based on extensive research on this topic, researchers have derived a curve of value-added time versus the number of parallel projects for engineers (from one to seven projects). The peak occurs between projects 1 and 2, where about 65% of the time an engineer spends is value added[1,2]. This tool applies to other product development functions as well.

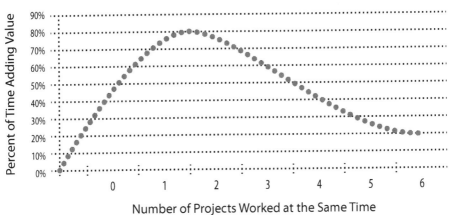

Value-Added Time vs. Number of Parallel Projects

The chart above is showing a graph of value-added time (time spent directly on the project) versus the number of projects.

Visualization

The Project Efficiency Chart below represents the extent to which project productivity can be negatively impacted by assigning team members to too many projects simultaneously. The vertical axis of the dotted curve shows the percent of time where the employee does added-value work. The horizontal axis is the number of projects a given individual is working on at the same time. The histogram, shown as bars expressing the percentage of individuals working on a range of projects, is labeled on the right hand vertical axis. As seen below, the majority of the team members were assigned to 3 or more projects, indicating that the percentage of value-added time was less than 60% in most cases, and, when the weighted average is computed, the average value-added time is only 58%. When the organization cut the number of projects from seven to five, the efficiency went up over 65%.

Project Efficiency Chart

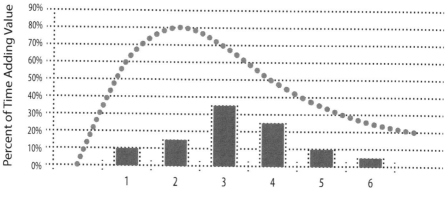

Percentage of Individuals working on a Given Number of Projects

What's New?

Project overloading is anything but new. It is becoming the biggest false economy and seems to be rapidly getting worse with the increasing speed of development, especially with SaaS (software as a service) and Web 2.0 development, where companies can push out releases daily. Directors want to optimize their resources by loading them up and having them do more on the priority list to satisfy the demanding executive suite. However, this is bad logic as it is neither more efficient, nor does it lead to higher throughput. The optimum load for a project team member (engineering/project management) is approximately two projects (one large and one small) - far from what we see in most organizations.

Benefits

- Provides a **visual map of overload**. Most managers are blind to the negative impact of overload.
- **Exposes overburdened functions**. If your goal is faster innovation and time-to-market, "more" is not better.
- Helps management **normalize workload to maximize efficiency** (and morale).
- **Incorporates best-practice metrics** that have external validity

Which Business Problems Does the Tool Solve?

Obviously, most organizations try to get the most out of the talent they have, but the tendency of managers, and especially executives, is to load up the team with too many projects. This tool helps to guide managers toward optimizing the product development throughput of their organizations.

What Else Should You Know?

You need to apply this method with some care. Projects come in all different degrees of complexity and, if the projects are very simple, this estimation method will break down. Some project team members are also more adept at handling more than one project at any given time, so you need to apply this tool judiciously with respect to the individual.

Case Study

WebCo, a company with about 200 contributors, was having trouble with morale as their projects kept slipping. An analysis of the root causes excluded the usual suspects (changing definitions, too few project managers, and too much technical risk). Many engineers complained of long days and nights along with demands by management that they attend many non-project-related meetings. The VP of engineering, wondering if they were spread too thin, did a quick tally of the organization and counted the number of projects (including management initiatives for process improvement, cost reduction, and the like). Here is what he found:

Number of Projects Managed	Percentage of Staff
1	10%
2	15%
3	35%
4	25%
5	10%
6	5%

Based on this analysis, the VP of engineering went to the management team and had them order their priorities, take two projects off the list, and put them in the "never" category. He also created a special projects organization where he handed a small group of people seven small projects that were dispersed across the organization and left unattended. The special projects manager applied the same logic to their portfolio and only worked on a subset of the seven projects to get greater speed and throughput. These changes moved the average down to two or fewer projects per team member across the organization. The management team was able within two months to see greater milestone achievement.

---

[1] Steven Wheelwright and Kim Clark, *Revolutionizing Product Development: Quantum Leaps in Speed, Efficiency, and Quality*, Free Press, 2011, pp. 88-91

[2] Jeffrey Liker and Walton Hancock, *Organizational Systems Barriers to Engineering Effectiveness*, IEEE Transactions on Engineering Management, EM-33 (2), 1986, pp. 82-91

Using Communities to Understand Customer Usage

Community Product Requirements Chart

What Is the Tool?

The Community Product Requirements Chart consist of stacked bars that summarize customer verbatim inputs, organized by category and distinguished by positive or negative ratings. It applies the methodologies of Voice of the Customer and contextual inquiry to communities. The objective of the tool is to provide you with customer insights and opportunities for innovation. The tool expands on one of the key concepts of the Voice of the Customer and contextual inquiry methodologies by capturing the customer's wants and needs as demonstrated in their environment of use. Through the use of internet-based communities and multimedia, you can capture the environment of use without incurring the time and expense of the team traveling to the customer.

You can use the Community Product Requirements Chart to enhance existing products or design and develop new products. You can increase innovation in your products by following the steps below:

1. Define the objective of the desired output. When engaging customers (or potential customers) and requesting their participation, it's critical that you clearly define the scope of the request. The value you derive from this tool is a better understanding of how customers will use your product. Failure to crisply define the objective will result in a lot of data that you probably won't know what to do with. Examples of objectives may include industrial design, packaging, or ease of use.

2. Define customer qualifications for participation. Inviting the most qualified voices will produce the best results. Some considerations for identifying the best participants may include early adopters, unhappy customers, or potential customers who are currently using a competitor's product.

3. Create a social space for sharing. If you are new to using social solutions in product development, but other departments such as marketing or customer support have established communities, then you can leverage that resource. If your customers are already talking to your company through social mediums, take advantage of that relationship. One of the key values of using a social solution is the "cross-talk" that will occur between the participants. This will provide much richer data than that produced by just bi-directional communication between you and customers.

4. Invite customers to participate in a time-bound exercise (ideally over two to three days). Request they fill out an NDA, and describe the benefits of participation.

5. Ask them to share photographs of how they are using your product, so you can actually see *their* usage. Also ask for textual input regarding what is going well or not well for them when they use your product.

6. Encourage discussion between participants.

7. At the end of the exercise, summarize the data to identify the high-value areas of focus for feature development.

8. Use the Community Product Requirements Chart, including photographic and textual data, to provide input to the product requirements process.

Visualization

The Community Product Requirements Chart below illustrates the verbatim inputs collected from a customer community. The vertical axis displays the number of positive and negative responses. The horizontal axis organizes the inputs by category, defined by the data table at the bottom. The data below, referenced in the case study later in this chapter, targets the product features and functionality that are most important to their target customers.

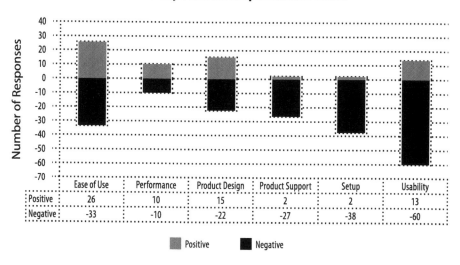

Community Product Requirements Chart

	Ease of Use	Performance	Product Design	Product Support	Setup	Usability
Positive	26	10	15	2	2	13
Negative	-33	-10	-22	-27	-38	-60

Positive   Negative

What's New?

Social collaboration solutions have become a critical tool for teams to share information and drive decision making. Research indicates that only about 14% of companies utilize social solutions, but 80% are expecting to in the next two years[1]. The companies that integrate these tools sooner than later can create an advantage over their competitors by sharpening their understanding of how customers want to use their products.

Benefits

- Ensures you are delivering a product with **high customer value**
- Saves time by **accelerating decision-making** based on customer input
- Helps you **avoid wasting time** on low-value features
- Drives **early customer support** of your product
- Is an **effective alternative** to the traditional Voice of the Customer and contextual inquiry methodologies

Which Business Problems Does the Tool Solve?

The Community Product Requirements Chart allows you to generate innovative solutions for new product designs by gathering the voice of the customer in a community setting. It is faster, cheaper, and richer than surveys or focus groups.

What Else Should You Know?

Many companies balk at implementing social solutions because they are unwilling to take the IP risks. However, this is a solved problem as organizations like Proctor & Gamble have good solutions to address intellectual property ownership[2]. It is also important to have the right number and type of customers participating in the process. Carefully selecting the community will increase the quality of the input, which leads to better and faster internal decision making.

Case Study

NetCo has decided to expand their network product offerings into the consumer market. While there is an opportunity to leverage their expertise from the enterprise market, they know this new market has challenges and opportunities that are unique to consumers. They also know that, if they don't get this right the first time, it will significantly impact their revenue target for this new line of business and considerably increase support costs. Bill, the EVP of engineering, wants to ensure that they deliver the best user experience possible on the first release of the product.

NetCo has used social solutions with their existing customers with good results, so he wants to utilize that experience to get the best customer usage data at the beginning of the development process. Bill asks Sarah, the product manager, to create a new social community and invite potential customers to provide input on their current network solutions with feedback on what works and what doesn't work.

Sarah has searched the discussion forums of competitive products for customers who are frustrated with their current network solutions. This search has resulted in the identification of about 100 qualified participants who have agreed to join NetCo's online community. Sarah has created a time-bound (three-day) forum and requested that the participants post photographs of their existing network solutions to the community. She has also encouraged them to provide input on what is working and not working and to build on the comments of others in the community. Although Sarah is moderating the community, she has also invited key members of the design team to participate and capture consumer feedback in real time.

Once Sarah has collected the photographic and textual data from the community, she summarizes it in a matrix. Sarah has assigned a customer number to each input, categorized the type of feedback, and given the input a rating of either positive (+) or negative (-). She has also noted each link on a wiki where the photograph can be viewed. From this data, Sarah creates the Community Product Requirements Chart. The table below represents an abridged version of the matrix. You would expect to collect 200-300 inputs from the community.

Categorized Summary of Community Product Requirements (Abridged)				
Photo	Customer ID	Customer Input	Category	Rating
photo1.jpg	45	Had a problem hooking up a Blu-ray player to Wi-Fi	Customer usage	
photo2.jpg	13	Everything works fine as long as I don't play World of Warcraft using wireless internet. Otherwise, the router crashes and then loses all the connections.	Customer usage	
photo3.jpg	93	The status lights are too bright. They are in the same room I sleep in, and they light up the whole room.	Product design	
photo4.jpg	81	The setup and installation were cumbersome. The install process would not finish when I used the CD because the self-diagnostic kept saying that it couldn't detect an internet connection.	Set up	
photo5.jpg	17	When I updated my router, it wiped everything and wouldn't take my password.	Usability	

Once summarized, the data is used to create the Community Product Requirements Chart as shown in the Visualiztion section above.

[1] Babson Executive Education and Mzinga. Social Software in Business Survey. http://www.mzinga.com/communities/resources.asp?pagen=1 (accessed November 2011)

[2] Larry Huston and Nabil Sakkab, *Connect and Develop: Inside Proctor & Gamble's New Model for Innovation*, Harvard Business Review, R0603C-PDF-ENG, March 2006

Organization

A classical definition of organization[1] by Wayne F. Cascio is "1) a group of people 2) who perform specialized tasks 3) that are coordinated 4) to enhance the value or utility 5) of some good or service 6) that is wanted by and provided to a set of customers or clients." We would expand this to include such aspects as communications, rewards and recognition, hiring, development, and performance management. However, in the context of this section, an organization is the people doing the work and how they impact others inside and outside the team.

Why Is This Section Important in Supporting Innovation and Time-to-market?

There is no argument that people and their relationships are incredibly important to innovation. How much more effective do you think your most productive engineer is in relation to your average engineer? Many organizations assert that they could easily be 10x or 100x more effective. Whether you think it is this high in your organization or not, no one can argue that individuals really make a huge difference. And on the downside, how many times have you had to deal with an individual in product development who was detrimental to the team? Even though some individuals have some significant technical skills to offer, they may fail to play well with the rest of the team and can cause disruption or significant delays.

We have found that the organization within the project team, the organization surrounding the team (including the management interface), and the large external environment (consisting of those in other divisions and departments and those outside the organization such as customers and partners) have a very big impact on product development effectiveness. We provide tools to optimize the organizational effectiveness of those three areas. The following chapters describe how to improve team effectiveness by clarifying who does what. The subsequent chapters outline methods for coping with the managers surrounding the development team and adjacent organizations. Finally, we address new topics around social networking technologies that help improve innovation.

Use Cases Where You Apply These Tools

In this section, the first two chapters concentrate on how you make decisions using the Circle Dot Chart and compose your team with the Project Team Wheel. You should use these tools at the beginning of a project if you are unclear on who has responsibility for top-level deliverables. You should use the Project Team Wheel at the beginning of the project as well to ensure that you have a clear team structure with established leadership and functions. The last team level tool shows how to optimize staffing by balancing ratios between key functions to avoid overload.

If you anticipate internal barriers to hinder your project, the second set of tools can be very useful. The Attitude Influence Map, is instrumental for product developers and change managers to understand who might be barriers and how to address them. You can apply the Change Impact Matrix in change management situations where you are rolling out a new system and need to ensure that you understand the ramifications of change. You should use this if you suspect that managers and politics might impact your project.

Finally, if you are contemplating the use of social technologies to increase innovation, the Social Innovation Readiness Scorecard can tell you if your organization is prepared to take on these new tools to enhance innovation. If you are fortunate enough to have begun this journey and have some initiatives already in place, the second tool, the Social Innovation Maturity Scorecard, can tell you how well you are doing against 10 key factors strongly correlated with social innovation success.

Chapter & Tool Listing

Title	Tool
Clarifying Responsibilities	Circle Dot Chart
Ensuring Project Teams Are Properly Staffed	Project Team Wheel
Optimizing Workloads Across Functions	Staffing Ratio Matrix
Eliminating Political Roadblocks	Attitude Influence Diagram
Understanding the Consequences of Changes	Change Impact Matrix
Applying Social Communities to Product Innovation	Social Innovation Readiness Scorecard
Improving Communities for Social Innovation	Social Innovation Maturity Scorecard

[1] Wayne F. Cascio, *Managing Human Resources: Productivity, Quality of Work Life*, Profits, McGraw-Hill, 8th edition, 2009

Clarifying Responsibilities
Circle Dot Chart

What Is the Tool?

Have you ever managed a project where it was not clear that someone was responsible for a deliverable until it was too late? The Circle Dot Chart solves this problem. It is a set of connected circles in a matrix framework that identifies key deliverables on the horizontal axis and key roles (or key individuals) on the vertical axis[1]. The chart consists of lines that represent the tasks going down the page and circles at the intersection of tasks and functional responsibilities. Specifically, open circles indicate that an individual function is involved, and filled circles represent the directly responsible individual (DRI) for a given deliverable. The DRI knows and agrees that he or she is responsible for the delivery of the task. Tasks with no circles mapped against a functional area indicate that the functional area is not involved in the task.

The process of creating a Circle Dot Chart for your project is very instructive. Initially, your project manager fills out a rough draft of the chart and then holds a review session with the team. They identify key tasks (approximately 5-15) from the project plan and put them in time sequence across the top of the chart. Next, they list the key functions responsible for delivering the program. It is important for you to differentiate between participating in a task and being ultimately responsible for delivering the task. Any functional group involved in a particular task is indicated by an open circle. The one function that is ultimately responsible for fulfilling the task is represented by a filled circle. All tasks must have one, and only one, directly responsible individual DRI.

The team should review the Circle Dot Chart early in the program. At the end of the review session, the functional representatives sign off on their various assignments. We advise you to store this document in the project team repository for easy access and review. When key tasks are coming due, you can quickly review who is responsible for their delivery. Most importantly, this is a living document, and, if responsibilities change, you must update the chart to reflect such change. You will find that the biggest value of this chart is the review session where the team discusses and agrees on the deliverables and who is responsible for them.

Visualization

The Circle Dot Chart illustrates the directly responsible individual and contributors for each key project deliverable. The vertical axis identifies the key functional team members, and the horizontal axis identifies the key project deliverables. With this tool, the team shares a common understanding of who contributes to, and who owns, the delivery of these key milestones. Because the business process user, change manager, finance and sales representatives are not involved in the core deliverables, they are not part of the core team and will only provide their input when needed. The training lead will be part of the core team later in the project.

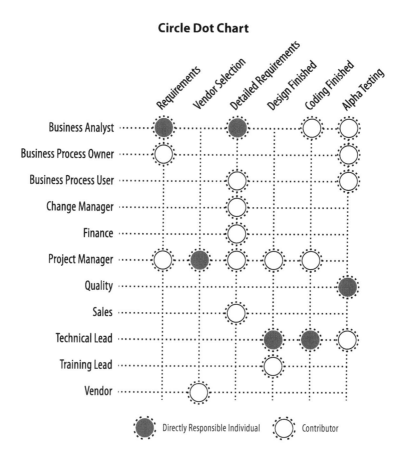

Circle Dot Chart

What's New?

The Circle Dot Chart will be incredibly useful to any team, but especially useful to teams that are globally dispersed. The clear responsibilities generated by this tool are very beneficial to the increasingly common outsourced development teams that are separated from the home office by time, distance, language, and culture.

Benefits

- Provides a **clear visual representation** of roles
- Helps **prevent missed deliverables** by clarifying who does what
- **Prevents wasted effort** resulting from having two people working on the same task
- Helps the team **share common understanding** of roles at the beginning of the project

Which Business Problems Does the Tool Solve?

Besides unclear requirements, unclear responsibilities are one of the leading causes of program delays. Providing the team with a crisp picture of key deliverables tied to key functions greatly reduces this problem.

What Else Should You Know?

In very large or very small programs, you should modify this tool accordingly to match the scope of the tasks at hand. For large projects, you can do this by having two levels of Circle Dot Charts - one overall and several others at sub-system levels. For example, in platform programs, there might be three second-level charts to cover the web, client, and device, and one overall (a total of four Circle Dot Charts). Sometimes there is also a need for even more clarity on tasks and specificity in roles. In this case, the three levels of Uninvolved, Involved, and Responsible are not sufficient, and you may need to add other roles such as Approves and Consults. There is a related technique called "CAIRO" that you can apply in this instance. CAIRO stands for Consults, Approves, Involved, Responsible, and Off (not involved).

Case Study

NetCo has set up a cross-functional team to address putting in place a new product process supported by product lifecycle management (PLM) software. They have developed a project charter and plan and identified the project manager, business analyst, business process owner, business process user, change manager, quality, finance, sales, technical lead, training lead, and an outside consulting team that will do much of the implementation and tweak the PLM software itself. The project manager has taken the first cut at a program plan and schedule and identified the project plan, key deliverables, and milestones. These include requirements, vendor selection, detailed requirements, design finished, coding finished, alpha testing, go live, beta, training, cut in, and post-mortem.

The project manager has done a rough cut of the Circle Dot Chart and presented it to the team (except the vendor) in a work session conducted at the headquarters, with several other sites dialing in via video conferencing. The project manager and the technical lead have agreed on modifying the circles representing vendor selection and coding finished, and they have published the chart on the team wiki.

[1] Ron LeFleur, "The Responsibility Matrix (Circle Dot Chart),"
http://www.ttoolboxes.ca/blog/index.cfm/2008/10/18/The-Responsibility-Matrix-Circle-Dot-Chart, accessed November 2011

Ensuring Project Teams are Properly Staffed

Project Team Wheel

What Is the Tool?

The Project Team Wheel is an analysis tool to clearly identify the team leadership, critical functions, and the specific individuals fulfilling these functions. This tool is a graphic snapshot that identifies, by name, the functional resources that you have assigned to the project. You structure the wheel as three concentric circles to differentiate between the project manager, the core team, and the extended team. The tool is scalable for large or small teams, and you can apply it to companies that reach outside the corporate walls to create project teams. In the case of smaller teams, you can use one circle. It is a powerful tool to quickly identify gaps in staffing and drive decision making to mitigate the associated risks.

Often you start projects with a suspicion that you don't have the skills you need to be successful, but, in the excitement of the kickoff, you suspend judgment. Invariably, something disrupts the project because you don't have the right resources in the right place at the right time. Inadequate staffing or unclear priorities across organizations often leave resource gaps on teams that lead to schedule slips. Managers often ignore complicated capacity-planning tools or find them obsolete, but the Project Team Wheel can be composed in minutes, communicated in hours, and resolved in days.

You can construct the Project Team Wheel in three short steps. First, the project manager creates an initial draft of the wheel by populating three concentric circles. In the innermost circle is the project manager for the program. You place their name in the circle below their title. The next circle is for the core team. Your project manager populates this circle with the four to ten critical functions that need to work intimately to get the product to market. These are the functions that would work more than half time on the effort and consider this project their number one priority. Your project manager lists these functions (often by marking up a similar Project Team Wheel) and the individuals who would work on them. The outermost circle represents the extended team and is appropriate for mid-sized and larger projects. You add here additional functions and individuals to supplement the core team and the interests that a given core team member represents. For example, you may have product marketing on the core team represent sales, sales operations, marketing, and training. You need to have these interests represented on the extended team as well.

The second step is to have your project manager review this diagram with the core team and ensure that they support their roles on the project and agree to represent their associated members on the extended team. This review would also look at omissions and the particular functions that you may need to re-staff because of their availability and/or the competency requirements of the project.

The last step is for your project manager to review this wheel with the management team to ensure that they agree with your structure and are ready to support your project with the people and functions you need.

Visualization

Below is the completed Project Team Wheel for the case study referenced later in this chapter. The inner circle identifies the project manager. The middle circle identifies the core team members, and the outer circle is the extended team. As illustrated below, the team has resource gaps in Software and Test. The project manager will escalate this information to the management team, indicating when this lack of resources will hit the critical path of the project.

Project Team Wheel

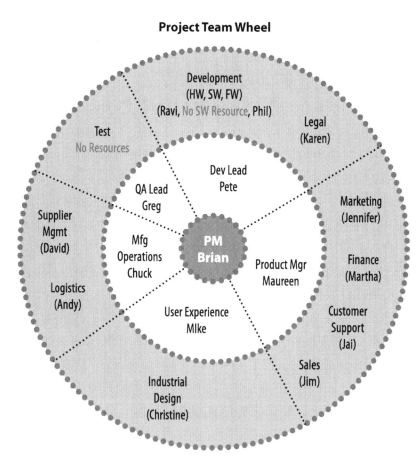

What's New?

The first trend you may have noticed is that organizations are doing more work offshore. The second trend you may have experienced is that management is delegating more tasks to project teams. Finally, if you are in a growing organization, you may have found that some functions have grown very quickly, leading to shortages of critical skills. For all of these reasons, creating a clear description of your team is more important than ever. The Project Team Wheel is one of the fastest ways to document and communicate the organizational needs of a program.

Benefits

- **Helps to ensure that team members are available** for your project
- Visually **identifies resource gaps** on a team
- **Describes the extended team functions** that a core team member represents
- **Minimizes surprises** (or project failure) attributed to not having the right resources in place

Which Business Problems Does the Tool Solve?

Often a root cause of project failures is the lack of adequate resources. Many resource management tools are complex and often not fully managed. The Project Team Wheel provides a compelling methodology for executives and project managers to quickly identify risk areas and address them before there is a significant impact on the team's schedule.

What Else Should You Know?

While this tool quickly identifies resource gaps and measures the degree to which you staff your projects, it does not evaluate the quality or effectiveness of the resources you assign. Three common examples that drive the effectiveness of assigned cross-functional resources are the level of skill, the point within the project when you assign the resource, and the level of distraction the resource experiences due to conflicting priorities. While these issues can have a measurable impact on a team's ability to deliver a project, you can manage the associated risks. It is relatively easy to keep the tool current over time to ensure that you identify and manage resource changes throughout the life of a project. This is accomplished by the project manager performing periodic updates to the wheel. And if a gap appears, they can raise it with their management.

Case Study

A program team in WebCo is responsible for delivering a next-generation product to market. The product consists of hardware, software, web, and mobile components, with the team geographically dispersed across three continents. As part of the program's kickoff, Brian, the project manager, constructs a Team Wheel to identify the resources available for this project and the gaps that he needs to manage. He also includes third-party offshore resources that have critical deliverables for the project.

To construct the Team Wheel, Brian does the following:

1. Identify core team members (typically – in addition to the program manager – a product manager, development lead, and QA lead, but can also include a design/UI lead and/or operations lead).

2. Identify both internal and external team members required to support the delivery of the product to market.

3. Populate the wheel with the name of each team member and their function.

4. Present the wheel to the core team, which includes Molly (the product manager) and three other members, for quick review.

5. Have the CEO (Rajiv), CMO (Ray), and CTO (Fred) review the wheel. They later ask Brian to swap out the current QA lead for another one (Greg).

Brian has indicated two areas where resources are not available. In this case, he discovers that the software and test teams are on a high priority customer escalation and are not available to work on the new product. This will impact the teams' ability to move forward with the project. Brian leads the core team members in a discussion to determine how to address this issue. They have decided to recommend to the CEO, Rajiv, that they go outside for QA and hire several experienced software contractors.

Optimizing Workloads Across Functions
Staffing Ratio Matrix

What Is the Tool?

The Staffing Ratio Matrix contains a summary of all the projects in a given function (as row headings), charted against the key functions found on a cross-functional team in order to give you insight into overloaded individuals and functional bottlenecks, so you can maximize speed. Typically in high tech businesses, these functions would be engineering, product management, project management, user experience, and quality. Clearly, you need to adapt this to your particular situation. These functions, besides engineering, are necessary for you to ship a product and would contribute to delays if you insufficiently staffed them.

The columns consist of a list of the names of the actual team members for each function for the projects on which each individual is working. Columns can also summarize this information so that an additional column consists of the total number of projects for each staff member. Each row consists of the staffing for a given project. The matrix should contain all the projects in your organization.

You can analyze and assess this summary in order to reduce overtaxed functions. The first step is to see how overloaded your individuals are. Often, the best producers are overloaded with an increasing number of projects until they break down given the workload. You can address these individual situations. The second step is to compare the average ratio in a given function to benchmarks. In our benchmarking work, the average ratio is one product manager per product family (or major product), and the average ratio for a project manager is 1.5 projects (a large and a small project).

Our interest in staffing ratios started with a benchmarking project for a Fortune 50 company that wanted to assess best practices in new product development. We benchmarked over a dozen companies all over the world and found that the most successful had one dedicated product manager per major product. Furthermore, these product managers only focused on inbound marketing - getting the voice of the customer into the organization. If the organization has more than one major product per product manager, it is very likely that these products will suffer delays because of incomplete and changing definition.

Similarly, others have performed research for the project management function and found that the effectiveness varied based on the number of projects they managed. The curve peaks between one and two projects[1]. We found the optimum workload for a project manager to be one large project and one small project. This allows the greatest throughput because, whenever there are activity gaps in larger programs, the project manager can turn his or her attention to smaller ones.

Visualization

The Staffing Ratio Matrix indicates the relative number of projects per function. The first column is the project name, the second is the number of development engineers working on that product, the next column names the product manager, and the next column summarizes the number of projects for each product manager. These columns are repeated for the critical functions. The last two rows summarize the workload ratio and the best in class ratio. The best in class ratio has been determined by observing many technology companies.

Staffing Ratio Matrix

Project	Engineers	Product Management	Ratio	Project Management	Ratio	User Experience	Ratio	Quality	Ratio
1 Blackbeard	32	Fred		Bob		Sarah		Andy	
2 Bluetooth	22	Fred		Bob		Sarah		Andy	2
3 Redhead	18	Fred		Bob		Sarah		John	
4 Silverfox	25	Fred		Bob	4	Sarah		John	2
5 White Prince	22	Fred		Mary		Sarah		Bill	1
6 White Queen	13	Fred		Mary		Sarah		Jill	
7 Mini Queen	4	Fred	7	Mary		Sarah		Jill	
8 Queen Three	11	Phil		Mary	4	Sarah	8	Jill	3
9 Bambi	13	Phil		Susan		Mindy		June	
10 BamBam	8	Phil		Susan		Mindy		June	
11 Fred	12	Phil		Susan	3	Mindy		June	3
12 Martha	5	Phil		Flo		Mindy		Janet	
13 Martha II	7	Phil		Flo		Mindy		Janet	
14 Martha III	5	Phil		Flo		Mindy		Janet	
15 Martha Junior	4	Phil	8	Flo	4	Mindy	7	Janet	4
Average Ratio		Eng/Proj	7.5	Proj/PdM	3.75	Proj/PjM	7.5	Proj/Qual	2.5
Best Practice			1		1.5		4		1.5

The above visualization shows how overloaded the product management function is in a division of NetCo. The case study shows that it is relatively easy to make a big change in the balance of product managers by shifting a couple of engineers into product management functions. We would also recommend that the division evaluate the project management function for overload. Although we don't have benchmark numbers for the networking industry for user experience and quality, they can determine these by competitive benchmarking.

What's New?

Successful outcomes require a team with all the skills needed to be successful. In many projects, there are skill shortages that can lead to programs that are late, over budget, or cancelled – and with the increased complexity of development, this is becoming more common than ever. Why is it a problem now? Our recession has caused many organizations to let go of many functions besides engineering, as they often consider them as support. Inevitably, business picks up and new projects begin, but they often lack the key resources surrounding engineering (product management, project management, user experience, and quality). A straight-forward tool that looks at staffing ratios – the ratio of the headcount of a skill to the number of projects – can help managers restore balance and execute more effectively.

Benefits

- Is a quick way to **cut through politics** whenever a manager asks for more people
- Makes **engineering much more efficient** by eliminating functional shortages
- **Improves project outcomes** because tasks are assigned to qualified workers (as opposed to using developers as a poor substitute for quality engineers)

Which Business Problems Does the Tool Solve?

You can greatly increase your throughput using the Staffing Ratio Matrix because it will ensure that you have skilled individuals working on key deliverables rather than engineers filling in and doing their best. This is a double win because you are no longer asking the engineering staff to work on non-engineering tasks, and the team also executes the tasks better since you have trained individuals working on them. In addition, you can accomplish this with no increase in budget. For example, if you redeploy a small number of open requisitions from engineering to these critical functions, you can solve most of the imbalance problems. Furthermore, if you transfer some engineers who would like to try different functions, you can improve the balance and create a better environment for those employees who would like to expand their experience.

What Else Should You Know?

There are many risks in applying this best-practice method since skill levels, job definitions, and projects vary so much in size and complexity. So, when you apply this method, you must factor in all these variables. When you are setting benchmarks on your own, the same concerns apply to the benchmark targets. For example, in benchmarking the Japanese consumer electronics companies, the best practice is one product manager per product. Their definition of product manager is very confined and limited only to inbound marketing (no promotion, advertising, or sales force management). This means that if you do not adjust their role when you change the ratio, and if you just look at headcount ratios and ignore the job descriptions included in the benchmark findings, you will only solve half the problem.

Case Study

A division of NetCo, which develops client software for its networking products, has approximately 200 engineers and 15 projects in its portfolio. The division was having trouble getting products out on time. Morale was low because the product definition was constantly changing and the engineering team was increasingly frustrated. They performed an analysis to look at the staffing ratios and discovered that there were approximately 7.5 products per product manager, while the best practice is one (large) product per product manager.

Rather than blowing the budget to hire 13 more product managers, the organization decided to convert three open requisitions from engineering into requisitions for product management. In addition, there were two engineers who wanted to get into product management, so they transferred them there and did not replace them. With minimal impact to the 200 engineers, the organization was effectively able to get closer to the benchmark numbers (from 7.5 products per product manager to three products per product manager). The organization decided to see how these changes would impact product development this year and which additional changes they would want to make next year.

---

[1] Steven Wheelwright and Kim Clark, *Revolutionizing Product Development: Quantum Leaps in Speed, Efficiency, and Quality*, Free Press, 2011

Eliminating Political Roadblocks
Attitude Influence Diagram

What Is the Tool?

The Attitude Influence Diagram is a scatter plot of your project's supporters and detractors to help you isolate and manage the key individuals who might impede your success. It provides a framework for you to plot individuals on the chart as bubbles, with their names and titles inside each bubble. One axis indicates how much they support your project (their attitude), and the other indicates their level of influence. Their influence is determined by a combination of their position in the organization and how much influence they command based on seniority, intellect, or knowledge. The size of the bubble indicates the difficulty in changing their position, where a larger bubble means that it will be more difficult for you to influence them.

The Attitude Influence Diagram is a subjective assessment; however, it is a very powerful tool to quickly identify those who might block your project. Applied early in the process, this tool will provide you with the opportunity to proactively manage detractors to ensure their concerns are addressed. In many cases, applying this tool will turn your detractors into supporters.

To create an Attitude Influence Diagram, generate a list of those who might impact your program. Plot them (typically on a white board) against the two axes. It is fairly easy to indicate their influence since more often than not it is their position in the organization. But think also of those individuals at the lower levels of the organization who have a high amount of influence (for example, while a senior architect may be an individual contributor, they can be well respected in the organization and their opinion is very influential). Their attitude is a bit harder to determine, so start by identifying the most negative and most positive persons. Then as you populate the chart, you can gauge comparisons against the two extremes. This is not a process that should include a large number of people from the project team. But you are best off if you do this with at least two people, so you can get a more balanced view of the situation.

By looking at the quadrant of high influence and negative attitude, you can focus your efforts and work on those individuals who are most likely to threaten your success. After isolating the detractors, you need to create a strategy to approach them and work through their concerns. This may include sending them an email asking for their input and requesting help, talking with them informally, or arranging a one-on-one meeting with them and another team member or with someone outside the team who is very influential to them.

Visualization

The diagram below shows the relative influence and attitudes of the key staff members who will be involved in the new project. The size of the bubble is a subjective indication of the difficulty in influencing the individual. The horizontal axis shows how negative or positive an individual is about this solution, and the vertical axis reflects their influence on the organization. The visualization below shows that work will be required on the engineering and IT managers to ensure project success since they are influential and have negative attitudes.

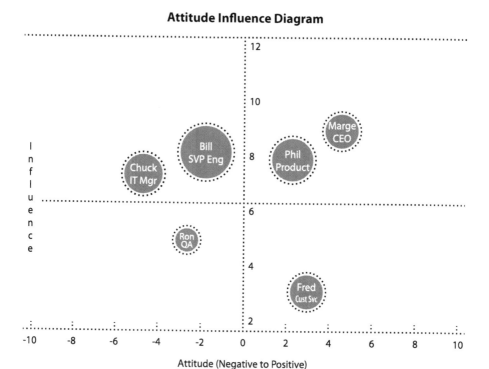

Attitude Influence Diagram

What's New?

Because management is now delegating more authority to teams, there is less top-down control and teams are now working more independently. In this environment, you need techniques to help your team be successful without invoking the management chain. This graphical technique allows you to predict who may block the success of your program. It helps you visualize supporters and detractors to pinpoint and eliminate blockers without resorting to escalating the problem through your management hierarchy.

Benefits

- Provides a visual political map to **clarify the landscape around your team**
- **Pinpoints blocking managers** who can disrupt your project
- Helps you **do something about it** before it affects the project
- Encourages you to **consider the project environment**

Which Business Problems Does the Tool Solve?

Frankly, we would like to say that your organization has no politics, but it does, and not everyone is aligned with your objectives. The result is that managers stifle innovation because they are risk averse and want to preserve the status quo. Political blockers in your organization can also increase time-to-market because their negative attitudes often result in behavior where they insist that you provide more and more evidence to convince them that the project should move forward.

We understand that you have limited time to work on politics. This graphical technique pinpoints people and their position so that you can use your time wisely. Provided you have a menu of solutions, you can start to act, drawing from proven change management techniques to deal with the influential, but negative individuals.

What Else Should You Know?

There is a big gap between knowing who your detractors are and eliminating their negative influence. Even more important than this graphical technique are the skills to influence outcomes. Sometimes it is challenging to agree on how to rank individuals, so, in addition to the recommendation of starting with the most positive and negative individuals, you can also do pairwise comparisons (e.g., comparing Bill with Frank and then Frank with Jill will help you find out how Bill and Jill compare). Some may feel this technique is political in itself, so be careful with how you select those who construct the diagram to ensure they use the information only to serve the success of the program.

Case Study

NetCo has kicked off a large web project to redesign the architecture to handle 25x more users, which requires new technologies and a new service provider (host). Though the CEO (Marge) supports the project, NetCo has not created a budget for it. In addition, the IT manager (Chuck) does not support switching to a new service provider, the QA manager (Ron) does not have the staff to support testing, both the EVP of engineering (Bill) and the CEO are not aligned on the technical approach, and finally the product manager (Phil) wants to include feature enhancements.

Richard, the head of the PMO, has enlisted two individuals in addition to himself to create a chart and determine how to make this web project successful. These individuals have created the graph, which shows clearly that Bill and Chuck are the two biggest detractors. Based on the fact that Richard knows Chuck and his past political behavior, he has a one-on-one with Marge and asks for her help. Given her support of the project, Richard is confident that her recommendations will be helpful. Indeed, she agrees to have a one-on-one meeting with Bill and pointedly asks him about his issues. Then she requests that Bill join the team to ensure that they address his issues and, in turn, asks for his support.

NetCo has decided that Chuck in IT will be an easier challenge to reverse. Richard takes this on personally and talks to Chuck. Because Chuck has brought up good critical issues during the session, Richard asks him to present these formally to the team. As the team addresses and resolves these issues, Chuck turns from a detractor to a supporter.

Understanding the Consequences of Changes

Change Impact Matrix

Barbara Shannon

What Is the Tool?

The Change Impact Matrix is a descriptive template that captures the details of what is going to change for everyone involved in your project. It aims to help the project team prepare for the change efforts and allows those impacted to get a feel for what will be happening to them. The Change Impact Matrix is a living tool where your project team derives benefit from both the initial creation and the updating of the matrix whenever new issues pop up and others are eliminated. The matrix is useful for presenting the project context to upper management when discussing the project status, schedule, and progress to plan, as it describes in a graphical and succinct way the drivers behind many of the program steps.

The program manager creates the Change Impact Matrix with the key core team members in the room. The best way to quickly complete the Change Impact Matrix is to assign your business owners from within affected functions to fill in the map for each role within their areas. These people can become your change ambassadors, and this exercise is a great way to ensure they fully understand the impact of your project on the people in their business areas.

You schedule a meeting for approximately 90 minutes where you review and modify the map in real time with the team. Not only will you find that the group process has improved the map's accuracy, but you will also see that the team has identified other functional areas that were missing in the draft. After the team reviews the Change Impact Matrix, executive management (or the executives in charge of oversight) should review it along with the project schedule. The program manager updates the map over time as issues get resolved or unanticipated issues arise.

You fill out the first major column of the table with the impacted group. It is best to start off with the most impacted group in terms of depth and frequency. The next two columns have to do with the impact of both technology and processes on the role/group. The final four columns in the matrix are subjective and the most important. You assess the estimated degree of change from the perspective of role, process, culture, and technology. A good group process for doing this change assessment is thumbs voting, where the members of the team filling out the matrix give thumbs up (high), thumbs sideways (medium), or thumbs down (low). The facilitator (project manager) then counts the most frequent thumb position. If there is dissention, the facilitator asks the biggest outliers to discuss their point of view. After limited discussion, the facilitator repeats the thumbs voting process and uses the majority opinion for the chart. The same process goes for subsequent roles.

However, understanding is only the first step to making change stick. If you have even one or two roles or functions that are medium or high on the map, you probably need to assign owners to manage training and communication work streams. Be sure these two work streams have capable leaders and detailed work plans and that the other project team members understand what they need to deliver to training and communication. If your communication leader does not participate in key team meetings, they will not have the message content they need to keep your stakeholders informed. If training does not have detailed as-is and to-be process flows, role descriptions, and changes to policy and procedures, your communication leader will not be able to develop training content and materials.

Visualization

Below is a Change Impact Matrix created to help convert a sales model from distributed to centralized, and ensure that there is adequate support in place with the new model, including the correct systems and roles. The second and third columns of this case study example are definitions of the Technology and Process changes. The four columns to the right indicate the magnitude of the impact of those two changes on a given individual, in four different areas.

The visualization shows that the team needs to develop detailed change management, communication, and training plans for supervisors and support teams. It also provides details regarding the specific technology and processes that they must cover in the change management and training work plans.

Change Impact Matrix

Role/Stakeholder Group	Technology	Processes	Role	Process	Culture	Tech
Supervisor	Telephony Implementation and Workforce Mgmt Processes	New reporting, queue mgmt, SLAs, new KPI, new tools	High	Medium	High	High
Mgmt and Support Teams	Telephony Implementation and Workforce Mgmt Processes	New reporting, queue mgmt, SLAs, new KPI, new tools, create new reporting	Medium	Medium	High	High

What's New?

As with the Attitude Influence Diagram, in this world of greater team autonomy, your team needs tools they can use by themselves because top management no longer micromanages as it once did. The team needs to be able to be more self-sufficient, and the Change Impact Matrix gives your team insight and clarity to implement change programs without needing top management at every juncture.

Sometimes you need a map. This one is both topographic and street level. It shows you the aerial, city-level, or street view of key change areas and provides a role-by-role description of how project-related changes will affect critical stakeholders.

Benefits

- Provides an **at-a-glance understanding** of high/medium/low change impacts
- Serves as a **discussion guide for planning** risk-mitigation activities
- **Informs project leaders** about areas requiring greater and lesser degrees of communication and training
- **Informs those impacted** about the degree of impact in advance of change

Which Business Problems Does the Tool Solve?

The success of most business projects hinges on the ability to implement change. Preparing the people who will be affected by this change is often the most difficult part of the initiative. A structured approach that focuses on the details can quickly target the roles that planned changes to process, hierarchy, and technology will affect. When your project has a limited budget, you may not have an assigned change manager. So this tool can help a project manager wear the dual hats of program manager and change manager.

What Else Should You Know?

First, make sure you cast a wide net and include as many functional areas as you can think of, and then add a few more! Second, make sure you invite senior people and deep thinkers to your review session. Finally, once you complete the Change Impact Matrix, be sure to use it regularly to get safely to your destination.

Case Study

NetCo has elected to change its business model from a distributed model with over 200 distribution centers to a centralized model using two call centers to process orders in one of its key divisions, the SME (Small and Medium Enterprise) Division. The transfer to the centralized model will take place in planned waves of a dozen local centers at a time. In some cases, the local center will remain open with a skeleton staff, while in others, the office will close and the local sales representatives and technicians will serve individuals and businesses out of their home offices and cars. They will call or fax orders to the call center, which will schedule equipment deliveries to businesses.

Here are the steps that Richard, the head of the PMO, has used to create the Change Impact Matrix:

1. Make a list of affected stakeholder groups. This includes all local offices, the call center, revenue collection (accounting), the sales organization, and technicians.

2. Assign an owner from each stakeholder group to complete the Change Impact Matrix. This includes the district leaders for all local offices and technicians, the call center manager, the AR director, and the VP of sales.

3. Develop criteria to define high/medium/low change impact status. Here is what Richard has arrived at for role impacts:

High	Job is eliminated or employee redeployed
Medium	Job role is substantially changed
Low	Job role is slightly changed

4. Have each owner complete and submit the template.

5. Have each owner recommend risk-mitigation activities for all high and medium areas.

Applying Social Communities to Product Innovation

Social Innovation Readiness Scorecard

What Is the Tool?

The Social Innovation Readiness Scorecard is a decision-making tool that provides executives and teams with an objective view of their organization's capability for successfully implementing social solutions (often called communities) to drive product innovation. The scorecard helps you determine whether or not your organization is prepared to launch a community by providing critical questions in 10 areas. These areas include the current use of social technologies outside of product development, level of management commitment, social community resource expertise, maturity of tools, and organizational structure to support the requirements for best-in-class application of social communities. The Social Innovation Readiness Scorecard allows you to identify the critical areas that many organizations overlook and the weak areas that you need to address prior to launching a social development initiative.

The scorecard itself is a spreadsheet that you develop with a group process. Typically, you would get a subset of your executive staff or senior directors together for a real-time meeting session (could be virtual) that would last one to two hours. You would first introduce the concept of communities and then instruct your group on the definition of the various dimensions of readiness. After the introduction, each person in the group individually fills out their scorecards, ranking the readiness of your organization without discussion. Then the facilitator collects all the scores and computes the average and standard deviation. In cases where the standard deviation is high, the facilitator asks some of the low-scoring individuals why they rated a dimension low and, similarly, why high-scoring individuals ranked it high. After comparing differences, your facilitator asks if anyone would like to change their ranking. This gives everyone an opportunity to vote based on a common understanding.

After performing the self-assessment, the facilitator creates an action plan by addressing the low scores in the scorecard. At this point, your organization will have a prioritized list of initiative areas to improve the readiness of your social innovation efforts.

Visualization

The chart below is a scorecard where each category is in the first column, the average score (1-5, low to high) from the team is in the second column, and the third column is the standard deviation from the team responses.

The case study at the end of the chapter has created the data in the scorecard below. The areas are shaded where the mean is below three on a five-point scale or the standard deviation is greater than one. You can communicate the ratings of each of the ten dimensions by giving examples of low versus high levels of performance for each dimension so that your team can provide more precise ratings.

Social Innovation Readiness Scorecard

Social Readiness Self Assessment	Mean	Std Dev
Maturity of social communities	2.9	0.7
Executive involvement	4.7	0.5
Defined objectives for social innovation	2.1	0.4
Social community expertise	1.9	0.8
Social technology investment	2.2	0.3
Maturity of your innovation process	4.3	0.7
Responsiveness to new ideas	3.7	0.5
Quality of idea repositories	3.1	0.4
Recognition systems	2.7	0.9
Reward systems	2.6	0.8
Average	**3.0**	

The score given to each category ranges from one to five, from low to high. In order to ensure the quality and uniformity of responses, the following table provides a definition of low to high for each category.

Category	Scale from Minimun to Maximum Degree
Maturity of your social communities	1 - Not used 2 - Pilot 3 - Only within a single function 4 - Cross-functional/whole company 5 - Inside and outside
Executive involvement	1 - None 2 - Functional support in one area 3 - Multiple areas 4 - C-Suite 5 - CEO and C-suite
Defined objectives of social innovation	1 - None 2 - Only strategic 3 - Strategically defined, no specific objectives 4 - Multiple objectives, minimally defined 5 - Multiple objectives, clearly defined

Social community expertise	1 - None 2 - Ad-hoc resource 3 - Expert resource 4 - Experts within a function 5 - Experts within a social center of excellence
Social technology investment	1 - None 2 - Consumer tools (Facebook/Twitter) 3 - SaaS-based collaboration tools, vendor identified 4 - SaaS-based tools utilized in a pilot project in company 5 - SaaS-based third-party tools utilized in production
Maturity of your innovation process	1 - None 2 - Not formal, but ad hoc 3 - Documented 4 - Documented and followed 5 - Center of excellence
Responsiveness to new ideas	1 - No response 2 - Occasional response to a few programs 3 - Consistent response 4 - Integrated response with rewards 5 - Consistent and major response
Quality of idea repositories	1 - Ad hoc 2 - Local/silos 3 - Site/functional 4 - Global 5 - Global & integrated with outside ideas
Recognition systems	1 - None 2 - Verbal acknowledgement 3 - Informal program including email 4 - Formal program 5 - Significant recognition such as office space
Reward systems	1 - None 2 - Small spot awards ($100 gifts) 3 - Large spot awards 4 - Resources to pursue innovation 5 - Both large awards and resources

What's New?

The most important aspect of applying social technologies to product innovation is the ability to create a "community" of technical thought leaders where they can share, build upon, and develop ideas. However, you need a methodology to prioritize and implement these solutions.

The application of new social technologies in the product development space is a new approach for companies, and we expect it to become an increasingly important methodology. Best practices in the area of social product innovation have emerged, and companies that apply these best practices are seeing good results. One common stumbling block for companies is trying to implement a social strategy without fully understanding how to optimize the process or how to integrate it into existing product development processes. The Social Innovation Readiness Scorecard solves this problem and allows the management team to provide their organization with their best chance at success.

Benefits

- Provides a new methodology for **accelerating innovation**
- **Identifies strengths and weaknesses** that will impact your probability of success
- Helps you **avoid mistakes** in the implementation process
- Creates a **framework for managing the implementation** of social solutions

Which Business Problems Does the Tool Solve?

Never has it been more important to innovate on an accelerated timeline. Applying social technology in the enterprise is not a fad. It has become a vital tool that goes way beyond its early applications in marketing, customer support, and training functions. The Social Innovation Readiness Scorecard will ensure that you get the best start by isolating key barriers and developing plans to overcome them in your first implementation of a social community for innovation.

What Else Should You Know?

When companies first applied social media to their enterprises, there was a big rush to implement a social strategy. Unfortunately, many companies stumbled because they jumped in before they really understood the framework they needed to be successful. They needed new tools, processes, roles & responsibilities, and decision-making models for successful implementation. The scorecard is based on research we have conducted on social innovation. The biggest barriers to successful implementation are:

- Lack of community management expertise
- Lack of a clear value proposition and what is in it for me (WIIFM)
- Missing system for taking ideas off the community and initiating them
- Insufficient reinforcements for participation

The Social Innovation Readiness Scorecard captures these and other potential barriers.

Case Study

NetCo has a strong R&D organization consisting of a total of 5,000 engineers and scientists located in five R&D centers around the world. The EVP of engineering, Bill, is not satisfied with the level of innovation that is coming from his team, nor does he think they are collaborating effectively. It is critical for NetCo to innovate faster in order to maintain their technology leadership in an increasingly more competitive market. Bill has heard rumblings about the benefits of using social solutions to drive innovation, but the marketing organization has had mixed results, and he doesn't want to drag the team through a new process without understanding its viability. He applies the Social Innovation Readiness Scorecard method to ensure that he and the executive team have asked the right questions and resolved the gaps before they invest their time in the process.

The results of the assessment indicate that there are three areas that he needs to work on before the rollout. He has enlisted the help of his lead program manager to drive the following initiatives with the goal of implementing a social community within three months:

- Implement a third-party social platform: internal tools for collaboration are not sufficient, and Bill doesn't want to use his limited technical resources to develop an in-house solution. He asks the lead program manager to investigate and implement a third-party SaaS (software as a service) solution.

- Identify a community manager: an unmanaged collaboration community can lead to sub-optimal results. It's a new skill set for the organization, and Bill cannot delegate it to someone who doesn't understand how to create and manage a vibrant community. He can either hire someone with this experience or work with the third-party solution provider to include this skill set until he can add someone permanently.

- Ensure that the community is working on a high-impact, but narrowly focused objective: communities that are too broadly focused will not create the highest-quality input. In addition, once the community loses its vibrancy, the team will stop participating.

Improving Communities for Social Innovation
Social Innovation Maturity Scorecard

What Is the Tool?

The Social Innovation Maturity Scorecard is a self-assessment of the maturity of innovation that organizations can drive by tapping the wisdom of the crowd, whether internal or external. While not all innovation is social, the best organizations are stimulating creativity by tapping into multiple minds and combining and refining ideas from communities. This scorecard method is straight-forward because it is a self-assessment with defined ratings along a scale of 10 dimensions that are good predictors of the strength and effectiveness of social innovation initiatives.

This process is identical to the one we discussed in the "Applying Social Communities to Product Innovation" chapter except that you are auditing the situation after implementation rather than before implementation. Since we would like each chapter to stand alone, we'll explain the process again below.

The scorecard itself is a spreadsheet that you develop with a group process. Typically, you would get a subset of your executive staff or senior directors together for a real-time meeting session (could be virtual) that would last one to two hours. You would first introduce the concept of communities and then instruct your group on the definition of the various dimensions of maturity. After the introduction, each person in the group individually fills out their scorecards, ranking the maturity of your organization without discussion. Then the facilitator collects all the scores and computes the average and standard deviation. In cases where the standard deviation is high, the facilitator asks some of the low-scoring individuals why they rated a dimension low and, similarly, why high-scoring individuals ranked it high. After comparing differences, your facilitator asks if anyone would like to change their ranking. This gives everyone an opportunity to vote based on a common understanding.

After performing the self-assessment, the facilitator creates an action plan by addressing the low scores in the scorecard. At this point, your organization will have a prioritized list of initiative areas to improve the maturity of your social innovation efforts.

Visualization

The case study at the end of the chapter has created the data in the scorecard below. The elements in the first column are based on our work with technology companies. The second and third columns contain the mean and standard deviation of a small number of scores collected by the executive staff going through this exercise. The areas where the mean is below three on a five-point scale or the standard deviation is greater than one are shaded. You can communicate the ratings of each of the 10 dimensions by giving examples of low versus high levels of performance for each dimension so that your team can provide more precise ratings.

Social Innovation Maturity Scorecard

Social Maturity Self Assessment	Mean	Std Dev
Maturity of your innovation on communities	3.2	0.5
Openness of external innovation efforts	1.1	0.8
Quality of idea repositories	3.7	0.5
Ease of locating innovation talent	3.5	0.4
Innovation technology investment	3.3	0.5
Executive involvement	1.9	1.5
Recognition systems	1.7	0.8
Reward systems	1.3	0.9
Maturity of your innovation process	3.1	0.4
Responsiveness to new ideas	4.3	0.4
Average	**2.7**	

The score given to each category ranges from one to five, from low to high. In order to ensure the quality and uniformity of responses, the following table provides a definition of low to high for each category. The right column indicates the standard deviation of the responses. The mean ratings range from one to five, where a rating of one would be low, a rating of three would be medium, and a rating of five would be high. The table above is a starting point for your organization to modify if they choose to change some definitions or add criteria.

Category	Scale from Minimun to Maximum Degree
Maturity of your innovation communities	1 - Not used 2 - Pilot 3 - Only within a single function 4 - Cross-functional/whole company 5 - Inside and outside
Openness of external innovation efforts	1 - Customer service only 2 - Enhancements 3 - Product features 4 - New product ideas 5 - Input on strategy
Quality of idea repositories	1 - Ad hoc 2 - Local/silos 3 - Site/functional 4 - Global 5 - Global & integrated with outside ideas
Ease of locating innovation talent	1 - None 2 - Informal 3 - Experts within a function 4 - Experts in innovation 5 - Experts with a track record of innovation
Innovation technology investment	1 - None 2 - Pilot status 3 - Production 4 - Multiple production sites 5 - Multiple vendors
Executive involvement	1 - None 2 - Functional support in one area 3 - Multiple areas 4 - C-suite 5 - CEO and C-suite
Recognition systems	1 - None 2 - Verbal acknowledgment 3 - Informal program including email 4 - Formal program 5 - Significant recognition such as office space
Reward systems	1 - None 2 - Small spot awards ($100 gifts) 3 - Large spot awards 4 - Resources to pursue innovation 5 - Both large awards and resources
Maturity of your innovation process	1 - None 2 - Not formal, but ad hoc 3 - Documented 4 - Documented and followed 5 - Center of excellence
Responsiveness to new ideas	1 - No response 2 - Occasional response to a few programs 3 - Consistent response 4 - Integrated response with rewards 5 - Consistent and major response

What's New?

What is new about the Social Innovation Maturity Scorecard is that you can use it to fine tune your implementation. The Social Innovation Maturity Scorecard helps you determine the maturity level relative to best practices in social innovation. This tool is also vendor agnostic, so you are not biased to a particular feature or practice that a solution provider offers. Finally, the scorecard leverages recent research and best practices in the social innovation field.

Benefits

- Provides very rapid and **low-cost feedback**
- Reveals opportunities for **innovation improvement**
- Improves social innovation, which can lead to **better engagement**
- **Borrows from best practices** and research, so you don't have to waste time yourself

Which Business Problems Does the Tool Solve?

Improved social innovation can help you get more innovative more quickly. By performing a gap analysis, the Social Innovation Maturity Scorecard motivates your organization to address the existing gaps. It also focuses the work on the biggest gaps, so you don't waste energy in the wrong areas. Finally, it may alert you to new areas of importance to leverage as you gain experience with communities, such as the development of systems to locate experts rapidly.

What Else Should You Know?

In any self-assessment tool, there are significant risks. The first is that you don't bring the right people to the table, so there are built-in biases that the facilitator needs to watch for. It is best to include some individuals who are neutral or from the executive ranks and not directly participating in the program. The second is that the real gaps may be off the list of the 10 maturity dimensions, so you need to apply common sense to cross-check the outcome of the scorecard.

Implementation is everything. Finding the gaps is very easy, but what is hard is finding the organizational will and energy to work on these more strategic areas. Having dedicated resources (such as the community manager) will help ensure action.

Case Study

NetCo has been concerned about innovation, and the CEO, Marge, has brought her extended staff together to discuss the matter. They have several initiatives on innovation, some involving outside facilitation and a couple of informal innovation communities that the SVP of engineering started several years ago. Marge is very keen to advance the company's use of social media. As NetCo has an external-facing blog, she believes that the company can do more in the area of social innovation. At the meeting, she selects a subset of her executive team – including Betty, the VP of HR, Bill, the EVP of engineering, and six other members – to get together and rapidly assess where they are and recommend where they should go.

The head of the effort is Betty, who uses the Social Innovation Maturity Scorecard as a tool to rapidly assess where the group is and discover the gaps quickly. She calls a 90-minute meeting the following week and tells the group that they will spend the first hour doing a self-assessment and the remaining time discussing action plans.

The group gets together, goes through the 10 criteria, and then quietly fills out their individual scorecards. When they are done, Betty records the results to a laptop connected to a data projector, so they can review them immediately. They find that the area of executive involvement has a large standard deviation of 1.5. Betty facilitates some discussion with the group and asks Bill, who gave the lowest score, and Mary, who gave the highest score, why they provided such ratings. When the team votes again, four of the eight members change their scores.

There are four areas that have a mean rating of less than 3.0. These are executive involvement, reward systems, recognition systems, and openness of external innovation efforts. The group agrees to focus on three of these areas first and defer work on the outside communities. Betty goes on to create a tiger team around reward and recognition systems, and Bill agrees to craft a communications plan and send it to Betty for review.

The team has been able to report back to the CEO in three weeks the results of the self-assessment and the progress they have already made on closing the gaps to improve social innovation.

Process

Process: Definition

Processes are the methodologies that describe how the organization will behave to support the strategy, management, and execution of its business objectives. Effective processes are characterized by clear definition, including why the organization is applying the process, what value it will deliver, and who will execute it.

The key to effective processes is to apply them at an appropriate level of rigor based on risk and complexity. This is a balancing act that requires the right judgment to ensure that you balance efficiency and bureaucracy. Most companies don't get this balance right.

We often find that companies are either over-indexed or under-indexed on process implementation. We typically see the former in larger companies where the amount of process applied throughout the entire development process is choking creativity, innovation, and speed. These companies typically consume an inordinate amount of time and resources just managing the process, with little consideration for the customer. The process is driving the business instead of the business dictating the process. Equally detrimental are those organizations that do not understand how well-placed and managed processes can accelerate creativity, innovation, and speed. We typically see this in fast-growing organizations that are challenged with expanding product lines and an increase in the number of project teams and team members, yet still try to manage much more complex businesses with the processes that worked on a much smaller scale.

To provide a recovery path for both scenarios, we coined the phrase "just right" process. The tools in this section demonstrate how you can apply best-practice processes to a broad range of companies and customize them to the appropriate level of complexity and risk. The extent to which you get this right (or wrong) will directly impact efficiency and morale.

Why Is This Section Important in Supporting Innovation and Time-to-market?

Processes are only as good as their application. If there is too much process, your team will be spending unnecessary time "dotting Is and crossing Ts" to conform, or they'll just work around it in an attempt to do their job. Alternatively, too little process burns the team out because mistakes are repeated. The ramifications of both conditions reverberate throughout the entire organization, and the time your team spends on managing inefficient processes replaces the opportunity for innovative thinking.

The processes that you clearly define, agree upon with the organization, and implement with the appropriate level of rigor, will free up your team to innovate and execute.

Use Cases Where You Apply These Tools

The graphical tools in this section will help you make better decisions faster. The first graphical tool will ensure that teams get a deeper understanding of when and how unplanned events negatively impact the program. The second tool will optimize new or existing processes that require broad cross-functional contribution. The third tool provides a fast, straightforward method for making group decisions when teams are faced with a large amount of data. The final set of tools provides methodologies for evaluating project trouble spots, including a gauge to determine how quickly you can expect to improve.

Chapter & Tool Listing

Title	Tool
Measuring the Impact of Unplanned Events	Event Timeline Generator
Clarifying Cross-Functional Handoffs	Four-Fields Map
Quickly Making Group Decisions	Dot Voting Chart
Making Better Decisions Faster	Project Escalation Map
Getting Beyond Symptoms to Causes	Root Cause Diagram
Making Sense of Qualitative Data	Affinity Diagram
Predicting the Speed of Improvement	Half-Life Diagram

Measuring the Impact of Unplanned Events
Event Timeline Generator

What Is the Tool?

The Event Timeline Generator is a powerful tool that allows teams to create a project timeline very quickly. You can generate and use the graph throughout the entire life of a project. Typically applied to a project's key milestones and deliverables, it's a great solution for smaller teams that don't use heavy project management software and want to quickly create and communicate the key events of a project.

The project manager completes the Event Timeline Generator with input from the cross-functional team (for example, after creating the Team PERT Chart). It is a customizable template that graphically displays events as a function of time. Planned events (typically the major milestones of your product development process) appear above the timeline. During the execution of the project, unplanned events are entered below the timeline.

Updating the timeline with unplanned events as they occur is important for two reasons. The first is that unplanned events can have a material impact on the speed and cost of delivering a project. What will be the impact if your lead architect resigns during the concept phase of the project, if you reassign key team members for two weeks to resolve a burning customer issue, or if an early risk buy of materials with a half-baked plan leaves you with yields too low to ramp up your project? The Event Timeline Generator allows you to memorialize these events as they occur and to make the best decisions to mitigate the risk that they generate.

The second is that, when you capture unplanned events, you create an effective tool for conducting mid-mortem reviews. This tool allows you to drive a root cause analysis and deeply understand the cause and true impact of unexpected changes. With this data, managers can make better decisions faster to avoid the impact of these changes or to help get the team back on track.

The Event Timeline Generator is also very useful at the completion of a project and can be used as the basis for the post-mortem process.

Visualization

Below is the application of the Event Timeline Generator. The horizontal axis is a function of time, mapping key project events. The vertical axis distinguishes between planned events, plotted above the horizontal axis, versus unplanned events, which are plotted below the horizontal axis. From the data below, the team has identified three key unplanned events that have impacted their ability to predictably deliver their project. They can now use this data to apply root cause analysis and corrective measures to bring the project back on track.

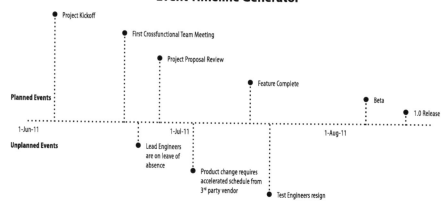

Event Timeline Generator

What's New?

The Event Timeline Generator allows you to very quickly generate a project timeline and update it with the unexpected. All projects experience change, but overlaying the expected with unexpected activities provides managers with a better picture of what is really going on.

Benefits

- Is a fast and easy way to **create and communicate a more robust project timeline**
- Quickly **flags the unplanned events** that cause schedule delays and increased costs
- **Triggers project learning** through mid- and post-mortems
- Provides a more **holistic view** of project execution
- Is an **excellent alternative for smaller teams** that do not use heavy scheduling software

Which Business Problems Does the Tool Solve?

The tool allows the team to create a graphical timeline very quickly. It also serves as the basis for project learning and incremental process improvement through flagging unplanned events and supporting root cause analysis.

What Else Should You Know?

The project information that you collect with the Event Timeline Generator is a snapshot in time. To optimize its effectiveness, you should update this tool on a regular basis. Moreover, while the tool identifies events that can push a project off course, it does not provide an analysis of the events. You must take additional steps to execute a root cause analysis followed by an action plan to mitigate the impact.

Case Study

CleanCo is delivering their first product to market. Bill, the marketing manager who is also acting as the project manager, is using a spreadsheet to track the project deliverables and timeline. The team is about one third of the way through the development process. Overall, they are making progress, but multiple changes have occurred that are beginning to impact the team's ability to deliver. First, the lead engineer is out on an unexpected one-month medical leave. Second, Wendy, the CEO, has requested a significant change in the project that has required them to find a new supplier. This has taken longer than expected and will soon be on the critical path. Third, two of the test engineers who were part-time contractors have left to work full-time for other companies. Bill knows that, individually and collectively, these issues are having a significant impact on the team's ability to meet their project commitments, but there is no holistic view of the impact relative to the overall project. He decides to construct a new project timeline using the Event Timeline Generator to graphically display the schedule and unplanned events and to plot future unplanned events, so the team can do a project root cause analysis when these major events occur.

Clarifying Cross-Functional Handoffs
Four-Fields Map

What Is the Tool?

Originated in Japan, the Four-Fields Map is a graphical technique most commonly applied to cross-functional processes. Unlike more traditional project planning methods that apply work breakdown structures, and critical path analyses that focus on what you do, the Four-Fields Map emphasizes the elements of tasks, teamwork, and quality, with a focus on how you do the work. Applications of this tool include supplier risk assessment and customer escalation process.

The tool describes the execution of a process across four areas or fields:

1. Phases: typically defined as the project phases in the product development process, these are discrete states over time that define where in the process the team is executing.

2. Tasks: the significant deliverables within the flow of the process.

3. People: the functions or individual(s) responsible for delivering the task within the phase. Typically, as the work flows through the process, the individual(s) assigned to the task will lead the process for the duration of that task.

4. Standards: the deliverables, documents, or specifications by which you will judge the quality of the tasks of the process.

You can construct a Four-Fields Map for product development using the following steps:

1. Identify a target process and define the process objective(s).

2. Create a flowchart of significant tasks and decisions points.

3. Map the tasks and decision points in a matrix of the product development phases against the team members responsible for their delivery. The tasks are connected to indicate the process flow over time.

4. For significant tasks, record the documented standard by which you can determine their quality (in the right-hand column).

Visualization

The Four-Fields Map[1] below illustrates the key cross-functional deliverables by phase for a procurement process. The process objective is stated at the top of the map. The map is organized on the vertical axis by contributing functions, and horizontally by development phase. The right column indicates the standard by which the quality of each deliverable will be evaluated.

Four-Fields Map

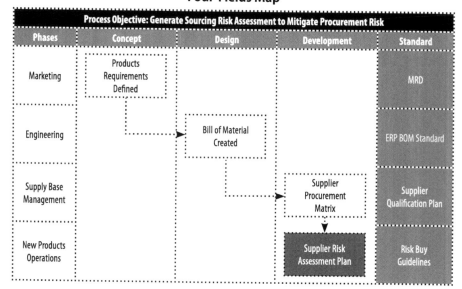

What's New?

This process is hardly new, but it is something that everyone should be aware of and apply frequently. For those who do use some form of process mapping, what's new is the concept of having a fourth field – the standard by which you judge the quality of a deliverable.

Benefits

- Is **very easy to create** because you start with a known structure
- **Drives process improvement** for sub-optimal processes
- Clarifies cross-functional handoffs to **avoid process gaps**
- Is a **consistent approach for executing the process** because it measures the quality of critical tasks against standards
- Ensures that stakeholders know ahead of time **how you will measure the success**

of the task

Which Business Problems Does the Tool Solve?

In a single view, decision makers and contributors can see the critical tasks of a process, the responsible individuals, and the criteria by which they will measure the successful outcome of a task.

What Else Should You Know?

The Four-Fields Map is a snapshot in time. As changes occur, you should update the tool to reflect the latest process information. Because the tool is focused on tasks, people, and standards, it does not include some of the elements of more traditional project management, including work breakdown structures, identification of the critical path, key dependencies, and oversight by the program manager. In most cases, you will want to use this process in critical areas in addition to more traditional tools for managing the overall project. Finally, while the process measures critical tasks against a standard, it does not ensure the quality of the standard. To get the best results, it is important to invest an appropriate amount of time to ensure that the standards support the effort of the team.

Case Study

NetCo is ramping up a new project with a significant amount of supplier risk. Tom, the VP of manufacturing operations, is concerned that the team does not have an adequate process to evaluate supplier risk prior to procuring components. His primary concerns are twofold: (1) many critical components are from a sole source; and (2) the product requires a new technology, and the primary supplier does not have high yields, indicating a quality problem. Tom knows that he has no room for error – delaying the schedule due to material availability, quality issues, or an increase in material costs would be fatal to the project. To lower the risk, he decides to implement a new process – a Sourcing Risk Assessment. Since this process requires cross-functional resources, and the team will execute it over multiple phases of the product development process, he asks them to use the Four-Fields Map to define and execute this critical process.

Tom assigns this activity to Bruce, the new product operations (NPO) manager. Bruce creates with the cross-functional team a Four-Fields Map to clearly identify the key stakeholders, their tasks throughout the phases of the process, and the standards by which they will evaluate the quality of the tasks.

[1] Nigel Wood, "Learning to See: How Does Your Supply Chain Function?" http://www.littoralis.info/iom/secure/assets/iom20041213.753113_41bde1a9d4ef.pdf, accessed October 2011

Quickly Making Group Decisions

Dot Voting Chart

What Is the Tool?

Dot Voting allows your teams to quickly make decisions when they are dealing with a large amount of data and need to either solve a specific problem or identify the most important elements. It is an equitable means for team members to hear each other and quickly reach consensus on prioritizing issues and identifying trends or major gaps. You can use this process in real time in a matter of minutes, as it requires no special data collection or synthesis tools.

When using the Dot Voting Chart in any type of problem-solving exercise, you start by creating a one-sentence descriptor of the problem you are solving. It is important, especially when there is a large amount of data, that the statement be well-defined in order to provide focus and yield the best information. Once you have defined the problem statement, the team will brainstorm ideas that support it. Each input represents a single idea or thought that is relevant to the defined problem.

There are several mediums you can use for Dot Voting, depending on the size and geographic dispersion of the team. In its simplest form, with a small team where everyone is in the same room, a facilitator (typically the program manager) can record ideas on a white board or flip board. Another alternative is to have the team use Post-it® Notes to collect inputs and then visually display them on a white board or flip board. The latter can be a more useful approach as it allows the team to easily group different ideas and avoid erasing and rewriting inputs. For geographically dispersed teams, there are SaaS (software as a service) solutions that support idea generation and clustering.

Once your facilitator has collected inputs, it's a good idea to review them to ensure that everyone understands what they have written. It's important before the voting begins to have a clear understanding of each input. A strong facilitator will need to ensure that the review doesn't turn into a debate on the merits of the inputs. This step is just to ensure clarity, not necessarily agreement.

When the input process is complete, it's time for your team to vote on the high-impact inputs that drive the agreed-upon problem statement. The facilitator provides each member of the team with an equal number of adhesive "dots", which they can purchase at any office-supply store. The number of dots they provide to each team member is discretionary (typically three or four) and normally depends on the number of team members and items that they created in the brainstorming session.

Your team members then "vote" with their dots by affixing them to the highest-impact elements. Your team members get to place no more than one dot per item. They vote silently to avoid cross-talk and influence over one another. Once they have completed the voting, the team is able to identify high-priority elements and trends. Based on the problem statement, the program manager can create an action plan to focus on the highest-impact items. It's a good idea to memorialize the outcome of the Dot Voting process by recording it with a digital camera.

Visualization

The Dot Voting Chart below shows 11 responses, captured on Post-it Notes, that answer the team's problem statement: "What are the key factors that led to the decision to eliminate desired features to ensure that the product was shipped in time for the holiday buying season?" The theme is at the top, the Post-it Notes are individual answers, and each dot represents a mark that was applied by a team member on a given answer. Additionally, it reflects the results of the team's Dot Voting to quickly determine the top three responses; which are: (1) slow decision-making to get agreed-upon list of reprioritized features, (2) early performance data required reprioritization of resources to resolve; and (3) quality problem at sole-source vendor created a delay in production. This process has accelerated the identification of the most impactful areas, and the team can focus from here on the next step of conducting a root cause analysis.

Dot Voting Chart

"What are the key factors that lead to the decision to eliminate desired features to ensure that product was shipped in time for holiday buying season?"

What's New?

Dot Voting is a process in which a team can take a large amount of data and quickly gain focus on the most relevant elements based on the team's shared analysis.

Benefits

- Provides a mechanism to **quickly organize and prioritize large amounts of data and key elements**
- **Leverages the collective wisdom** of the team
- Provides an equitable way for all team members to **hear each other and have accountability** in prioritizing key issues
- Provides focus to **ensure the team is working on the most critical issues**
- **Provides context between all the data** generated in a brainstorming session and the most important elements using a graphical representation
- Ties problem solving to a pragmatic tool that **leads to high-priority action**

Which Business Problems Does the Tool Solve?

In team environments, it is sometimes difficult to reach a conclusion. This tool can quickly get a team into alignment and ensure that they do not waste time choosing and deciding on an issue.

What Else Should You Know?

You cannot apply Dot Voting to all types of data analysis or decision making. But when you need to get concurrence on the "big picture" and there is a large amount of data within the team, it will provide focus to move the team in the right direction and can serve as a basis for a more detailed analysis.

Case Study

WebCo has just launched the latest version of their flagship product, barely in time for the holiday buying season. In order to make the deadline and ensure that the product was in stores, the company had to drop features, air-ship the product from the manufacturer, and do last-minute updates of the firmware. With the product out the door, the team is now conducting a post-mortem to understand all the unplanned events that forced them to make these costly decisions.

The program manager directs the post-mortem meeting, and the leads from the cross-functional team (product management, industrial design, user experience, software and hardware engineering, QA, manufacturing, supply chain management, finance, and customer support) are in attendance. The team has formulated the following organizing question: "What are the key factors that led to the decision to eliminate desired features to ensure that the product was shipped in time for the holiday buying season?" Each team member comes to the meeting with project materials to participate in a fact-based discussion that addresses the agreed-upon theme.

The program manager leads the brainstorming session by capturing inputs from the team members and writing them on Post-it® Notes affixed to a white board. Once they complete the brainstorming, the program manager gives each member of the team three dots to vote on their top items of highest impact. They do the voting silently so as to not influence one another.

Making Better Decisions Faster
Project Escalation Map

What Is the Tool?

The Project Escalation Map is a tool that clarifies the boundaries and channels of decision making throughout an organization. Designed around the concept of a core project team, the Project Escalation Map displays a path for allowing the core team to make decisions at the lowest point in the organization and to minimize the time it takes to escalate decisions that are beyond their scope of authority.

You can create the tool in a spreadsheet format and easily customize it based on your organizational structure. As you use the Project Escalation Map over time, you can fine-tune the level of detail based on the complexity of the project.

For larger organizations with a project management office or a lead project manager who is responsible for overseeing multiple project managers, it is best to develop the Project Escalation Map framework to ensure a consistent process across the entire organization. There may be exceptions to the process on a project-by-project basis, but in most cases, a consistent application of the Project Escalation Map will yield the fastest decision making.

The project manager constructs the Project Escalation Map in four steps:

1. Define decision categories. These can include areas such as finance, staffing, tools, and technical features/functionality. When defining the categories, be mindful of the right balance in the number of categories based on the complexity of your organization. You don't want too many to overburden the process, and too few will not provide a meaningful escalation path.

2. In each category, determine the appropriate path of escalation by functional responsibility. Start at the lowest level in the organization, typically an individual contributor. Some decision categories can have parallel communications (functional and cross-functional).

3. Define the key organizational contributors and their decision authority. This can vary based on the size and complexity of the project. In some cases, there will be dual communication paths (functional and project) to ensure rapid decision making.

4. Socialize and gain agreement on the categories, decision authority, and escalation path.

Visualization

The Project Escalation Map provides the responsibility and communication path for effective decision-making. The left column categorizes the type of decision. The middle column provides specific types of decsions that map into the categories. And the right column shows the path the escalation should follow from Individual Contributor to the C-suite. Not all decisions will go to the top of the organization. The scope and impact of the decision will determine what level of authority is required.

Project Escalation Map

Decision Category	Decision Type	Escalation Path
Product Features/Functionality	Feature	IC:FL:PM:CT/FD:BU:CMO
Staffing	Schedule, Cost	IC:FL:PM/FD:CT:BU
Change Management	Process	IC:PM:CT
Product Cost	Cost	IC:FL:PM:CT/FD:BU:CFO:COO
Legal	Legal	IC:FL:PM:GC
Customer Service	Schedule, Cost	IC:FL:PM:BU:CMO
Process Improvement	Schedule, Cost	IC:PM:PMO

Legend	Organizational Contributor	Decision Authority
IC	Functional Individual Contributor	Functional Execution
FL	Functional Lead	Functional Delivery
PM	Project Manager	Project Delivery
CT	Cross-Functional Project Team	Cross-Functional Execution
FD	Functional Director (or VP)	Functional Budget
BU	Business Unit Lead	BU Delivery
GC	General Counsel	Legal Compliance
PMO	Project Management Office (or PM Leadership)	Cross-Project Delivery
CMO	Chief Marketing Officer	Customer Experience
COO	Chief Operating Officer	Corporate Execution
CFO	Chief Financial Officer	Corporate Financial Performance
CEO	Chief Executive Officer	Corporate Delivery

What's New?

With the movement of most organizations toward core teams in product development, there is often a gap in how decisions are made outside the team's span of control. The Project Escalation Map provides the team with a clear line of sight to who can resolve problems and what they need to do to make that happen.

Benefits

- **Saves time and energy** by providing a clear escalation path for decision-making
- **Educates new team members** on how to make decisions quickly
- **Minimizes delays** in delivering products to market
- **Drives accountability** in the decision-making process

Which Business Problems Does the Tool Solve?

One of the biggest obstacles to improving time-to-market is struggling with decision making when teams are stalled. The Project Escalation Map is an effective tool that documents who decides what, given a certain set of conditions.

What Else Should You Know?

The Project Escalation Map will only be effective if all the levels of the organization agree on the process. When a team escalates an issue, the next level of the management team needs to be prepared to quickly provide guidance. In addition, the quality of the team determines the effectiveness of the tool. You need to have strong team members throughout the organization who are willing to be responsible for driving decisions and have the good judgment to carry out those decisions within their scope of authority.

Case Study

NetCo is working on the next release of their flagship product, which will be available at their annual conference in seven months. The hardware team is in the early stages of the design phase and is making progress. Although NetCo has assigned two members from the firmware team to the project, they have yet to begin work. One of the hardware engineers, Frank, is concerned that if they don't get engagement soon, they will fall behind. In a conversation with one of his colleagues in firmware, he learns that they are still working on an update for the last release and will not be available for another three weeks. Frank can't resolve this issue on his own, so he relies on the team's Project Escalation Map to resolve this issue as soon as possible.

By using the map above, Frank determines that this is a staffing issue that is about to impact the project schedule. He escalates the issue to his functional lead, Sharon, who is also a member of the cross-functional project team. She doesn't have authority over the firmware engineers, so she informs the project manager of the resource conflict. She also takes the issue to her functional director, Jack, who manages all of the engineering teams in the business unit. Jack decides to keep one of the firmware engineers on their current work and to split the time of the second engineer in order to provide staffing for the new project.

Getting Beyond Symptoms to Causes
Root Cause Diagram

What Is the Tool?

The Root Cause Diagram is a framework to support the discovery of the ultimate cause of an outcome. Also known as the fishbone diagram or Ishikawa diagram, it is the diagram representation of the outcome of a method where individuals or groups systematically attempt to determine the set of the most fundamental, detailed, specific, and fact-based causes that led to a specific outcome. The application of the Root Cause Diagram is flexible and straightforward, and you can accomplish it in two one-hour sessions.

There are four ordered steps to determine root causes. The first step in this process is identifying the problem and creating a clear problem statement. It is critical to get this step right, as the solution that results from this process will be so much easier to implement if the problem is well-defined. We will use code names to illustrate this concept. These code names describe projects under development, all relating to similar animals found in Northern California – Banana Slug, Salamander, and Tadpole.

Example problem statements might be:

- What are the root causes of our changing requirements for the Banana Slug project?
- What are the root causes of our project Salamander's time-to-market delays?
- What are the root causes that led our support costs to be so high in our last Tadpole release?

The second step is to list out standard categories for the root causes of the problem statement. This helps your team get started and ensures that they cover the range of possibilities. Examples of categories could be a combination of people, processes, environment, or management. If this is too limiting, more detailed categories such as functional groups (marketing, design quality, etc.), sequence (kickoff, concept, design, and testing), or general hypotheses in the case of high support costs (design, manufacturing, shipping, etc.) may be more suitable. The problem statement determines the types of categories you should apply.

The third step is to then ask why each category led to the outcome. You repeat this process (also known as the 5 Whys) up to five times. It is this step where teams often apply the Ishikawa diagram or cause-and-effect diagram, with the problem statement at the head of the fishbone describing the effect. However, this diagram is often cumbersome to create in a computerized form or in distributed work team sessions. A better and more adaptable approach is to use the Root Cause Diagram, utilizing a spreadsheet to categorize the various root causes into primary and secondary. Often, the third step is the most difficult, and this is where you can use the Root Cause Diagram to quickly group processes to make rapid progress. The fourth step is to come to an agreement on the most likely root cause (or causes).

The best way to implement the Root Cause Diagram is with a cross-functional team and a facilitator. You can carry out the first session, covering steps one through three, in an hour if the participants come in prepared to analyze the topic and the facilitator is prepared to lead the team. You can conduct the fourth step in a second meeting since it involves data collection and analysis.

Visualization

Below is an application of the Root Cause Diagram. The left column organizes data by functional category. The remaining columns display the progress of asking the question "Why?" to get to the ultimate root cause. The diagram below, based on the details of the case study referenced later in this chapter, shows that the team used a spreadsheet to facilitate a root cause analysis for a project that had a longer-than-planned test phase. In this diagram, the team did not ask why five times. Instead, they went at least two levels deep to get to the root causes of the long test phase. Because the team had deep understanding of the likely impact of some of the root causes, they did not go to the Why #3 level on many of the Why #2s, After creating the diagram, the team collected data and selected the late involvement of the quality organization as the leading root cause.

Root Cause Diagram

Category	Why #1	Why #2	Why #3
Engineering	Lack of unit testing		
		Lack of training	
		Lack of process steps	
			Management does not support process
		Unclear exit criteria	
	Unclear functional specifications		
Marketing	Changing product definition		
Software Quality Assurance	Insufficient staff		
		Manager left 1/2 way through test phase	
	Low morale		
		Overworked	
		Underappreciated	
	Insufficient automation		
		Budget does not allow automation effort	
	Lack of comprehensive test plan		
		Quality joins team at feature-complete milestone	

Process	Quality joins team after design phase		
	Process is not enforced so engineering does not follow procedures		
	Executives change features at last minute		
	Release criteria is not clear		
Technology	Lack of test automation		
		Lack of budget	
		Lack of top management support	
	Bug tracking system insufficient		

What's New?

The application of the scientific method is now in favor in Silicon Valley after a period where engineering managers believed in more tribal, fast, and loose product development methods. In addition, given the fact that things change so rapidly, managers often believe studying the past is irrelevant. However, both of these assumptions cannot be further from the truth. Teams should never make the same mistake twice, but we see them do it all the time!

Benefits

- Saves time because the **team does not repeat mistakes**. This tool ensures that the team will manage the actual root causes, not just the symptoms.

- **Minimizes re-evaluation** because the team does the formal exercise once at the beginning of a project.

- **Generates consensus** because it is a cross-functional effort, and all the participants collaborate on the key takeaways of the process.

- Prevents swirling changes in direction because it drives thoughtful and **fact-based decision-making**.

- Allows for **easy collaboration with distributed teams** because it is in a spreadsheet format.

Which Business Problems Does the Tool Solve?

This tool facilitates fact-based decision making and evidence-based management. The fishbone diagram is a nice way of diagramming the discussion of an exercise to determine root causes, but it is difficult to share after the meetings, or real time in a distributed meeting. By using a spreadsheet tool, it facilitates the use of root cause documentation because it is trivial to share and archive.

What Else Should You Know?

Root cause analysis is only as good as the people who are participating in it, so you need to carefully select the team. The process also depends on how you craft the problem statement - the more specific the problem statement, the better. We cannot stress enough the need for a cross-functional team because there are so many unintentional functional blind spots. In addition, by using a cross-functional approach, you will likely get broad-based support and buy-in for the conclusions. Finally, you will need sufficient time and deep thinking to get to the heart of the matter - superficial or general root causes have limited benefit.

Case Study

CleanCo just kicked off a project to develop a new product. Unfortunately, the last project didn't go so well because the time-to-market was too long. The team and their management wanted to improve time-to-market for this effort. The problem with the last project lay in the test phase. The new team got together with several old team members to do the root cause analysis, which took two sessions and some work between sessions. The team generated the following problem statement: "What were the root causes of the long test phase in project Jupiter?" The team decided that the primary root cause areas should be functional areas along with process and technology. Therefore, the primary root cause categories were:

- Engineering
- Marketing
- Software Quality Assurance
- Process
- Technology

The team received the theme and categories in the first meeting so they could get right to work. The quality manager facilitated the process as he had training in root cause analysis. The team created the diagram above during the first session and, at the end of the session, performed Dot Voting to pick out the top three root causes for data collection. The quality manager, along with the engineering manager, started collecting data to present it to the team a week later in order to confirm the hypothesis of the top three root causes. Then the team spent the second session brainstorming solutions and came up with the primary recommendation to bring QA into the Concept Review process, so they would be an integral part of the team and could anticipate test requirements early.

[1] Eric Ries, *The Lean Startup*, Crown Business Press, 2011

Making Sense of Qualitative Data
Affinity Diagram

What Is the Tool?

The Affinity Diagram, also referred to as the Language Analysis or KJ Diagram, is a graphical technique for analyzing verbal data. This diagram, which consists of groups and hierarchies of sentences, provides one of the fastest ways to reach consensus on any complex situation. The steps to create an Affinity Diagram start with a question that the team would like to answer. Note that "theme" and "question" are often used interchangeably. Often the questions that the team uses to frame Affinity Diagrams are in the form of "what" questions. For example, "What are the root causes that led to the delay of our last platform release?"

To apply the Affinity Diagram tool, the project manager gets the team together and asks them to review this question and discuss it. It is critical that the question be well-defined and not too broad. Then, using 3" x 3" adhesive-backed notes, each team member writes a complete sentence that addresses the question. It is best to use black markers and write in all capitals, so the notes are easy to read from a distance. The sentences on the notes should be fact based and very granular (detailed and specific). Avoid using absolute words such as "always" or "never", and provide a specific description of the fact you need to express, quantifying it if possible. For example, a relevant point for the theme above might be, "The lead architect left the company three weeks after the start of the project and was not replaced."

The goal is to fill out 20-25 notes. Typically, these are three to four notes for each person in a group of seven. The group arranges the notes on a flip-chart paper in groups of three or fewer (one note is called a "lone wolf"). This grouping process typically proceeds apace until at some point it naturally stops. If there's a conflict, the project manager will jump in and try to form the right grouping with the consensus of discussion, but this should happen infrequently. Then the team adds a title statement to each group of two or three notes that expresses its essence.

After this step, the team performs an omissions check where they step back and look at the big picture to see if they neglected to write down any key elements that address the theme. Often, some of the biggest insights come from this step, so it is important to include this check. Once this step is complete, the team will do a second grouping using the same process, including a grouping of title statements. The end result is a diagram that shows the most relevant items along with the top three groups based on group voting. You can also add a final step by applying arrows to represent cause and effect between the groupings. For posterity, it's a good idea to take a photograph of the diagram and convert it into a presentation diagram.

Visualization

Below is an application of an Affinity Diagram. Each of the boxes represent data that was collected on a Post-it Note. The diagram illustrates how the data is grouped and labeled. The white notes represent the data that was generated in answering the organizing question. The shaded note is the synthesis of the notes located directly below it. The capitalized text describes the synthesis of the groupings, and the arrows indicate cause and effect between the groupings.

Affinity Diagram

"What are the root causes that prevented the wireframe from being completed on schedule, that would be relevant to the next phase of the project?"

WebCo Next Gen Product

MARGINALIZED PLANNING, EXECUTION AND RESOURCES
CREATED DELAYS IN THE PROJECT SCHEDULE

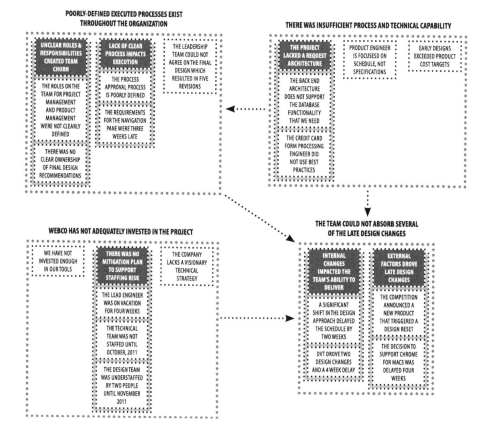

What's New?

The Affinity Diagram is a technique that synthesizes ideas and data and quickly facilitates team consensus. It is not a new technique, but most teams do not apply the process, as they don't understand the value of language data and how it can drive a more meaningful analysis. Based on a well-defined question, the Affinity Diagram is a fact-based analysis of a problem that provides deeper insight and helps you consider the problem in a different way, which will lead you to more effective solutions.

Benefits

- Provides a visual representation of **the key drivers that answer a particular theme**
- Is **very quick to execute,** so two to three hours should be sufficient
- **Forms consensus rapidly** without iteration and without a lot of arguing
- **Supports a wide range of major functions** within the organization including product development, research, process improvement, strategy, and product planning and requirements

Which Business Problems Does the Tool Solve?

Many issues in real life and business are not quantitative, but rather involve words that are qualitative. This tool effectively deals with language data and is one of the best techniques for establishing future direction and providing vision or guidance on how to move forward in a collective fashion by getting everyone on the same page with a common vision. It helps answer questions such as:

- What are the reasons that led the quality of the last release to be below our standards?
- What is the root cause for the sales performance to be below forecast?
- What are the issues that prevented the rapid adoption of the new customer requirements management system?

What Else Should You Know?

For this to be a good process, you need the right people in the room. If you don't have a skilled cross-functional team, you won't get the kind of deep insight that this technique can offer. This is especially true if you are missing some of the key functional groups involved in the theme. In addition, a precise phrasing of the theme question is very important, as described above. Finally, it's a common mistake to write responses to the theme that are too general. This process works well when the individual fact statements are as detailed as possible.

Case Study

WebCo was developing their next-generation product. The design team finally got the initial wireframe signed off, but it took a really long time – much longer than the project team expected. Brian, the project manager, wanted to know how to speed up the project by learning from this last phase, so he decided to use this technique to understand what caused the delay and to prevent it from happening again. The theme question was, "What are the root causes that prevented the wireframe from being completed on schedule?" He brought together the five key members who worked on the project for a three-hour session. They discussed the theme and slightly changed it to add "that would be relevant to the next phase of the project" to focus on what they could influence going forward. Brian handed out notes to each team member to answer the theme question.

Each team member wrote down three to four reasons for the delay, each on a separate note. Then all five members silently grouped them together, creating groups of one, two, or three notes. For each group of two or three, they created a label. Once they completed the group labeling, they did one more grouping and again labeled groups of two or three. After discussing the results of the groupings, the team generated a final label that answered the initial question. They then presented the resulting diagram to the management team.

The diagram shows that the key drivers for the schedule delay are in the areas of process, resources, change management, and investment. The team wants to focus on the area that would be most relevant for the next phase and thus decided that the highest impact was in the area of process definition and execution. Because a key driver was the lack of clarity in cross-functional responsibilities, the team decided to complete a Function Phase Matrix to quickly gain alignment. In addition, the management team agreed that the project team needed crisper decision making and, therefore, implemented an Out-of-Bounds process, so they could quickly resolve issues that prevented the team from executing to the plan of record.

Predicting the Speed of Improvement
Half-Life Diagram

What Is the Tool?

The Half-Life Diagram predicts how fast you can expect to improve or make an impact in your organization depending on organizational and technical complexity. This prediction provides a continuous estimate of progress, against which you can plot your own actual progress and course correct if you see an early deviation.

The Half-Life Diagram consists of an equation and a graphical plot of expected improvement over time. It uses estimated degrees of technical and organizational complexity (high, middle, and low) as an input to the model, and then estimates the rate of improvement based on a study of nearly 100 similar projects[1].

This tool generates a target curve over time that a project team can use to gauge its progress. Although most of the applications of this tool come from process improvement and change management initiatives, there are many other areas where you can apply it – either exactly as stated or in spirit. Based on technical and organizational complexity inputs, the output is a continuous graph that shows the projected improvement. The Half-Life Diagram gets its name from the time period needed to get to 50% improvement, which is called the "half-life" since it is the time required to cut errors by half (or, if you are an optimist, to improve things by a factor of two). Therefore, if the time period for 50% improvement is one month, after four months you will accumulate a total improvement rate of 93.75% .

Teams and management can use this tool to track interim progress and take action before it is too late. Below is a table that shows how the improvement half-life varies by technical and organizational complexity.

Project Type	Examples	Typical Half-Life	Minimum Half-Life	Maximum Half-Life
Unifunctional	Market Requirements Document	3	0-1	6
Cross-Functional	New Product Cycle Time	9	6-18	12-48
Multi-Entity	Vendor Quality	18	12-18	24-48

Visualization

The Half-Life Diagram illustrates how fast a company can expect to improve over time. The vertical access measures the degree of compliance, and the horizontal axis is a function of time. The curve provides the trajectory for change. In the case study below, the team expects it will take about four months to fully adopt the new MRD process.

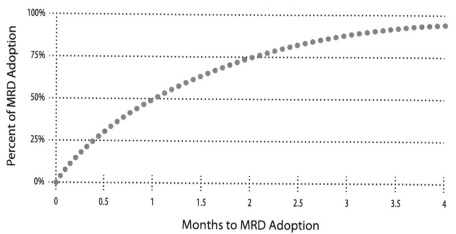

What's New?

While the Half-Life Diagram has been available for many years, most companies don't apply it because it has not been publicized. The Half-Life Diagram is the best way to determine the feasible rate of improvement based on complexity.

Benefits

- ◎ Provides a visual target curve to **manage expected versus actual improvement**
- ◎ Does not require a lot of upfront planning, and **teams can quickly apply it** to most improvement opportunities
- ◎ Is a unique tool that **provides a consistent, fact-based guideline** to achieve improvement goals
- ◎ **Forces teams to continuously monitor progress** and compare against a standard, so they don't lose sight of the pathway to improvement

Which Business Problems Does the Tool Solve?

The Half-Life Diagram provides a target for improvement, which ultimately accelerates most improvement initiatives. It also reinforces a data-driven and evidence-based culture that aligns teams and management. Finally, it provides a weekly or monthly reporting tool for progress reporting if required.

What Else Should You Know?

This estimation technique is most useful for process improvements and change management projects commonly found in IT, HR, and R&D. First, check to see if this applies to your initiative. Second, if you can forecast improvement based on external events (like monthly cycles or an IT system going live), use those more contextual estimates. The Half-Life Diagram is used when there is no better way of estimating improvement rates. Finally, organizational and technical complexity is hard to guess; use estimates and then perform a test of reasonableness on the predicted half-life. If it seems off (or way off), don't throw out the method – just adjust the half-life estimate.

Case Study

WebCo has recently adopted a new Market Requirements Document (MRD) process, but has not yet rolled it out. This organization has about 200 members and has little experience with process rollouts, so they do not have an adoption baseline they can show to management. The team knows from experience that simply declaring that they must do something new doesn't work, so they have planned many training sessions and created a support wiki. But how fast should they expect adoption?

Precise Definition

How many out of the total projects listed as being in the investigation phase in weekly and monthly updates have an MRD? The team considers a project to have an MRD if they identify a specific document as fulfilling that function, regardless of its title.

Sample Baseline

An adoption baseline is difficult to measure without identifying project phases. Based on the sampling from "slotting exercises" (which place projects on a standard timeline with standard milestones where it is possible to "slot" their relative location on the timeline), roughly 0% of the projects are likely to have MRDs at the start. The goal is to reach 90% MRD adoption.

Half-Life

The half-life is three months (example: time to go from the initial value of 0% to half the gap of 100% of that value, or 50%). However, in this situation where the organization is relatively small and located in the same physical location, the half-life would be closer to one month. The team agrees to use this assumption and adjust it in two weeks if it is off base.

Baseline Value

Currently 0% of projects have MRDs. In order to increase the adoption baseline value, the organization needs to provide an example MRD and then ensure that all teams flowing through the product definition stage use this new form. The teams are then checked at the next management review to ensure compliance.

[1] Arthur Schneiderman, "Setting Quality Goals," Quality Progress, April 1988

Appendix

Tool Combinations to Drive Focused Solutions

Innovate Products Faster was written so that each tool within a chapter can stand alone. While you can gain value from individual tools, you can gain more by combining them to address specific problem areas. Below are examples of common issues that prevent your organization from maximizing innovation and time-to-market.

Increasing Product Delivery Predictability

Managing Change

Minimizing Risk

Creating Effective Teams

Innovating Products Using Social Communities

Innovation Process

Process Improvement

Post-Mortems

Metrics

Product Definition

Project Management

Increasing Product Delivery Predictability

Improving predictability requires improving two fundamental work processes – how to plan work and how to execute it. We have comprehensive tools to address these two areas. The best tools for setting schedules are the Team PERT Chart and Schedule Estimating Matrices. In order to execute work effectively, you need to manage change and exceptions quickly, which the Boundary Conditions Diagram and the Out-of-Bounds Check will help you do.

Section	Tool	Chapter Title
Introduction	Product Innovation Process	Innovating Products Faster
Management	Boundary Conditions Diagram	Setting Project Boundary Conditions
Management	Out-of-Bounds Check	How to Quickly Get Projects Back on Track
Execution	Lite and Precise Schedule Estimating Matrices	Quickly Estimating Accurate Project Schedules / Precisely Estimating Accurate Project Schedules
Execution	Team PERT Chart	Reducing Schedule Through Teamwork
Execution	Task Burn Down Chart	Tracking Real-Time Progress
Execution	Deliverable Hit Rate Chart	Managing the Speed of Deliverables
Execution	Schedule Prediction Accuracy Chart	Early Indicator of Schedule Risk
Organization	Staffing Ratio Matrix	Optimizing Workloads Across Functions

Managing Change

By far, one of the biggest factors for an organization to be able to quickly innovate and deliver is effectively managing change. Managing change requires you to clearly set goals and change management vehicles to move the organization from the current state to the desired state.

Section	Tool	Chapter Title
Strategy	Technology Roadmap	Anticipating Future Technology Trends
Strategy	Product Roadmap	Clarifying Your Product Direction
Organization	Attitude Influence Diagram	Eliminating Political Roadblocks
Organization	Change Impact Matrix	Understanding the Consequences of Changes
Process	Project Escalation Map	Making Better Decisions Faster

Minimizing Risk

Risk is inherent to any product development initiative; however, you can significantly reduce risks by anticipating them with the Risk Mind Map and monitoring them with the Risk Management Matrix. The Product Radar Chart can give you a comprehensive view of the overall product attributes from a business perspective, to help you minimize market risk.

Section	Tool	Chapter Title
Strategy	Product Radar Chart	Making Intelligent Product Tradeoffs
Management	Risk Mind Map	Comprehensive Overview of Major Risks
Management	Risk Management Matrix	Anticipating and Mitigating Risks

Creating Effective Teams

Optimizing a team's ability to execute is critical in accelerating product delivery. You have the best chance of poising your team for success by applying tools that help clarify the roles and responsibilities of the team (often called the core team), guide the team when changes happen, and staff them sufficiently.

Section	Tool	Chapter Title
Introduction	Core Team Roles and Responsibilities	High-Performance Teams
Management	Nine-step Initiative Plan	Getting Teams off to a Good Start
Management	Function Phase Matrix	Avoiding Gaps Across Functions
Process	Project Escalation Map	Making Better Decisions Faster
Execution	Project Efficiency Chart	Optimizing Workloads Within a Function
Organization	Project Team Wheel	Ensuring Project Teams Are Properly Staffed

Innovating Products Using Social Communities

There is a sharp rise in the use of social solutions to drive product innovation. With this emerging technology, organizations are not only able to easily harness the innovative thinking of their teams, but they are also able to get closer to the customer. Getting started is the hardest part, and you may wish to try the Social Innovation Readiness Scorecard first, followed by the Maturity Scorecard and the Community Product Requirements Chart.

Section	Tool	Chapter Title
Strategy	Social Community Matrix	Getting the Most out of Social Communities
Organization	Social Innovation Maturity Scorecard	Improving Communities for Social Innovation
Organization	Social Innovation Readiness Scorecard	Applying Social Communities to Product Innovation
Execution	Community Product Requirements Chart	Using Communities to Understand Customer Usage

Innovation Process

Although innovation tips abound throughout the book, there are two tools that concentrate their focus on innovation improvement. The Product Innovation Process provides an overall framework for the entire product creation lifecycle, and the Comprehensive Innovation Map describes the key process that facilitates innovation.

Section	Tool	Chapter Title
Introduction	Product Innovation Process	Innovating Products Faster
Strategy	Comprehensive Innovation Map	Creating Better Innovations Faster

Process Improvement

Reducing time-to-market is a goal you cannot achieve overnight. Process improvement throughout the development lifecycle will help you take the waste out of the system. The Four-Fields Map is a process-mapping tool that allows you to see problems in product development. The Root Cause Diagram and the Affinity Diagram help you analyze these problems, and the Half-Life Diagram allows you to understand how fast you will be able to improve.

Section	Tool	Chapter Title
Process	Four-Fields Map	Clarifying Cross-Functional Handoffs
Process	Root Cause Diagram	Getting Beyond Symptoms to Causes
Process	Affinity Diagram	Making Sense of Qualitative Data
Process	Half-Life Diagram	Predicting the Speed of Improvement
Process	Event Timeline Generator	Measuring the Impact of Unplanned Events
Process	Dot Voting Chart	Quickly Making Group Decisions

Post-Mortems

Post-mortems are retrospective processes held at the end of a program. The following tools will help you structure a post-mortem session to analyze problems and synthesize common themes.

Section	Tool	Chapter Title
Process	Event Timeline Generator	Measuring the Impact of Unplanned Events
Process	Dot Voting Chart	Quickly Making Group Decisions
Process	Root Cause Diagram	Getting Beyond Symptoms to Causes
Process	Affinity Diagram	Making Sense of Qualitative Data

Metrics

Metrics are useful for comparing yourself against your competitors (usually involving results metrics) and guiding improvement (usually involving predictive metrics). The tools below will help you benchmark your organization (Staffing Ratio Matrix and Project Efficiency Chart) and allow you to formulate predictive metrics for improvement (Predictive Metrics Tree).

Section	Tool	Chapter Title
Management	Predictive Metrics Tree	Rapid Indicators for Early Warning
Organization	Staffing Ratio Matrix	Optimizing Workloads Across Functions
Execution	Project Efficiency Chart	Optimizing Workloads Within a Function
Execution	Schedule Prediction Accuracy Chart	Early Indicator of Schedule Risk
Execution	Deliverable Hit Rate Chart	Managing the Speed of Deliverables

Product Definition

Product definition is the most common source of delays in time-to-market, yet taking the time to define your products can lead to the greatest innovations. The tools below provide suggestions for improving both product definition and time-to-market as well as leveraging product platforms.

Section	Tool	Chapter Title
Strategy	Product Roadmap	Clarifying Your Product Definition
Strategy	Product Radar Chart	Making Intelligent Product Tradeoffs
Strategy	Platform Derivative Chart	Maximizing the Value of Your Platform
Management	Requirements Management Matrix	Accelerating Innovative Product Definitions

Project Management

Often project management is one of the most critical functions in delivering a project on time and on budget. The tools below help project managers look at their own efficiency (Project Efficiency Chart), describe their role (Project Team Wheel and Function Phase Matrix), plan better (PIEmatrix Multi-Project Map and Team PERT Chart), and get projects back on track (Out-of-Bounds Check).

Section	Tool	Chapter Title
Management	PIEmatrix Multi-Project Map	Project Portfolio at a Glance
Management	Function Phase Matrix	Avoiding Gaps Across Functions
Management	Boundary Conditions Diagram	Setting Project Boundary Conditions
Management	Out-of-Bounds Check	How to Quickly Get Projects Back on Track
Execution	Project Efficiency Chart	Optimizing Workloads Within a Function
Execution	Team PERT Chart	Reducing Schedule Through Teamwork
Organization	Project Team Wheel	Ensuring Project Teams are Properly Staffed

Importance of Time-to-Market

Stan DeMarta

In today's market, the timely launch of a product is more critical than ever before. For example, in the consumer business, product lifecycles are short (six to 18 months). In addition, all major brick-and-mortar retail chains have very well-defined (and published) reset cycles of one or two times a year where they will take on new products to put on the store shelves.

To illustrate the importance of time-to-market and the cost of delaying, we use the following graphs.

In Figure 1, we depict a very simplistic product sales lifecycle. This assumes the product as designed has a market life of about one year. The important characteristic to point out is the launch date. This date is internally driven. That is, the company controls this date based on various factors such as development schedule, manufacturing throughput, and filled distribution channels.

The second point of interest is the end-of-life (EOL) period (in this example from 3/1/2011 to 6/1/2011). This is the period in which the product as introduced is no longer retaining its sales level. This could be due to a number of factors, such as the loss of market share to competitive products and the end of life of key components used in the product. In almost all cases, external factors (i.e., factors outside the control of the company) dictate the EOL period.

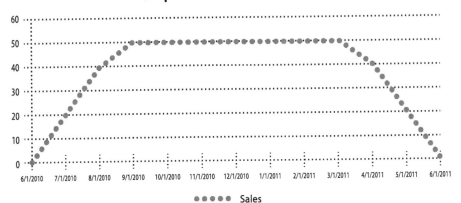

Figure 1

In Figure 2, we see the effects of delaying the launch. Since the launch date is internally driven, it is possible to move it out (one month in this example). However, unlike what many may think, the end-of-life date doesn't move out with it. Since the end of life is externally driven, the date stays the same. In this example, the difference in the areas under the two curves (the red area) is lost sales.

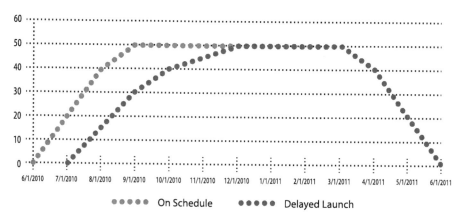

Figure 2

Figure 3 depicts a more extreme case where a retail reset is missed. We see that the effects of delaying the launch are drastic, in part because the company could never fill some of the distribution channels. Again in this example, the difference in the areas under the two curves (the red area) is lost sales. At this point, the company should look carefully at the cost of development to determine if the product has actually netted a profit.

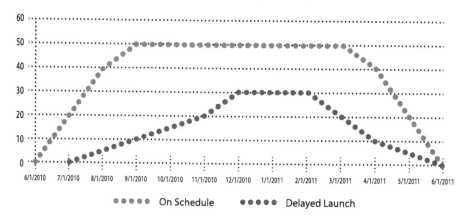

Figure 3

What does all this tell us?

- At the highest level, delaying launch dates not only leads to additional NRE costs, but more importantly can significantly reduce sales.

- To combat this, you should thoroughly understand the minimum product configuration needed to help drive the product features with the appropriate launch date. This is actually harder to do than most product managers think. Too many times, product managers add features and claim they are required, but in reality they're willing to ship without them. This causes delays or the loss of major features.

- Don't take extra time to design the prefect product up front.
    - First, as the graphs above show, you will miss out on substantial revenue.
    - Second, only the market knows what the perfect product is, and you're better off getting the first version into consumers' hands early to learn from them.

- Plan a phased approach to introducing new product features from the beginning. When companies don't do this, one of two things happens:
    1. They do everything to meet the original schedule and end up having some features completed, some features partially completed, and others not started. Without the original plan, the mix of completed features may not be the most important. A plan helps prioritize the feature set for the release.
    2. They miss the launch date and end up in the scenario depicted in Figure 2.

Online Tools Available for Download

The application of these tools will help you significantly improve your ability to increase innovation and accelerate time-to-market. We also know that getting started can be difficult in fast-moving organizations, so we have provided on line a set of tools that you can download and apply immediately.

In working with clients, we've found that the implementation of these tools can be accelerated by providing relevant examples in a software format that can be easily customized. To support you in their application, we are providing examples of the tools on our website. To download a copy that you can customize for your own projects, please visit www.tcgen.com/book/tools/

About the Authors

John Carter

John Carter has been a CEO, founder, and widely-respected advisor to technology firms over his 35-year career. As the principal of TCGen, Inc., he has advised technology firms large and small in strategy and operations (Cisco, NetApp, Sausalito Audio, and Teachscape) and currently serves on the Board of Directors of Cirrus Logic (CRUS). John has raised private equity to successfully execute a rollup in the consumer electronics sector and assumed the roles of CEO and CTO at Chelix, Livescribe, and Klipsch.

He was the founder and principal of Boston-based Product Development Consulting, Inc. (PDC), a leading organization in advising Fortune 500 companies in the areas of research, development, and marketing. He has consulted to high-technology companies over the last 15 years, working with clients such as Apple, Cisco, Hewlett-Packard, IBM, and 3M. He has been a member of the faculty at Case Western's Executive program and an invited speaker at MIT and Stanford University. John has served as an advisor to the International Association of Product Development, the Gordon Institute, and the Management Roundtable.

Before starting PDC, John was the chief engineer of Bose Corporation where he managed the development of technologies such as the Acoustic Wave Music System, Wave Radio, Lifestyle Home Theatre, Noise-Reduction Headphones, and others. He was one of the initial contributors to Bose's entry into the automobile OEM business and led the product and business development of Bose's patented noise-reduction technology for the military market.

He earned his MS in electrical engineering from the Massachusetts Institute of Technology and a BS in engineering from Harvey Mudd College in Claremont, CA.

Jeanne Bradford

Jeanne Bradford has been a business and technology leader across a broad range of high-tech companies over her 25-year career. She has led global organizations for some of the industry's leading companies including Apple, Cisco, and AOL, to deliver compelling products and technologies.

While at Apple, she led the re-architecture of Apple's new product development process, resulting in faster time-to-market for the Macintosh product lines and a process that Apple used to deliver the iPhone and iPad. Additionally, she was a key leader in the teams responsible for delivering simultaneous global launches as well as global manufacturing readiness and customer feedback programs. During her tenure at AOL, Jeanne was a member of the technical leadership team that executed AOL's ad revenue strategy (aol.com). Her expertise in transforming product roadmaps into action and in leading complex global initiatives contributed to the successful implementation of this strategic initiative.

As a results-driven leader, Jeanne has a proven track record in building lean global teams that deliver high value. Her strengths and expertise include product roadmap execution, remote development, product development best practices, and program management. She is a frequent industry speaker in the areas of product development best practices and the emerging use of social technologies for social product innovation.

She earned an MBA from Santa Clara University and a BA in mathematics from the University of Missouri in Columbia, MO.

Contributors

We have been privileged to work with some of the industry's best thought leaders in the area of innovation and product development. We are grateful for their generous contributions to this book and have provided their websites, so you can learn more about their work.

Paul Dandurand, CEO and Founder
PIEmatrix
www.piematrix.com

Paul Dandurand has a background in starting and growing companies. Prior to PIEmatrix, he was the co-founder of FocusFrame where he wore multiple hats, including those of co-president and director. He helped position FocusFrame as the market leader with process methodology differentiation. FocusFrame was sold to Hexaware in 2006. He acquired his enterprise project management experience at Ernst & Young (now Capgemini) and Siebel Systems. At PIEmatrix, Paul promotes innovation and customer value.

Dr. Scott S. Elliott, Principal and Founder
TechZecs LLC
www.techzecs.com

Scott Elliott is well-known globally for his experience in high-tech and electronics design, manufacturing, and supply chain management. With over 25 years of engineering, management, and consulting experience, Scott brings unique, practical insight to all aspects of technology business, including business strategy alignment, supply chain management, world-class manufacturing, and R&D management. Scott has served on four boards of directors, holds two patents, and has authored or co-authored over 50 publications on technology, R&D, and technology and business management. He is a frequent speaker and instructor on management, technologies, trends, and best practices in electronics and optical design and manufacturing.

Wayne Mackey, Principal
Product Development Consulting, Inc.
www.pdcinc.com

Wayne Mackey's expertise is grounded in more than 20 years of hands-on management of large engineering, manufacturing, and procurement organizations. His management consulting focuses on product/service development, especially in the areas of collaborative design, metrics, supply chain management, and business strategy implementation. A natural change agent and leader, he has counseled Fortune 500 companies, major universities (Stanford, MIT, and Carnegie Mellon), and government agencies in product development, supply chain management, and the rapid implementation of enterprise-wide change. He has also worked as a senior scientist, materials operations manager, program manager, engineering manager, and systems engineering manager.

Sheila Mello, Managing Partner
Product Development Consulting, Inc.
www.pdcinc.com

Sheila Mello is the author of the bestselling book *Customer-Centric Product Definition: The Key to Great Product Development* and co-author of *Value Innovation Portfolio Management: Achieving Double-Digit Growth Through Customer Value.* Sheila is the managing partner of Product Development Consulting, Inc. (PDC) and is a widely known, well-respected expert in the field of product development. Her clients benefit from her many years of executive and hands-on experience in product development, software, hardware, engineering, marketing, quality, manufacturing, sales, and service. Sheila has done extensive research on processes for defining customer requirements and is an expert in helping companies implement and institutionalize market-driven product definition programs. Before joining PDC, Sheila held director and vice-president positions at Bolt, Beranek & Newman, Wang Laboratories, Palladian Software, and Distribution Management Systems and was a principal consultant with Arthur D. Little, Inc.

Barbara Shannon, Founding Partner
TSG - The Shannon Group
www.shannon-solutions.com

Barbara Shannon has over 20 years of experience in guiding senior executives through business transformation initiatives. Her deep expertise includes change management, program management, and strategic planning. She has partnered with the senior executives of Hewlett-Packard, Lockheed Martin, Applied Materials, and many other Fortune 100 and 500 companies to help them set new growth strategies, implement post-merger integration plans, define and deploy new business models, and manage large-scale system implementations. Prior to founding TSG, Barbara was a senior executive at Deloitte Consulting. She is a guest lecturer at the Wharton School and has written and taught case studies for conferences, consulting firms, and executive education, including Gartner's Business Process Re-engineering Conference and the Wharton MBA program.

Jeffrey Harkness, Founder
Hark Digital
www.hark.bz

Jeffrey Harkness has established an international reputation in web design and development via his first design consultancy, Diesel Design. Since 1998, he has worked to launch hundreds of online ventures, chaired industry conferences, and displayed his work in a host of design competitions. Currently based in Vermont, Jeffrey has more recently focused his attention on a handful of innovative companies' digital presence. He holds a degree from Wesleyan University and has spoken around the country on the state of design and the creative process.

References

Babson Executive Education and Mzinga. Social Software in Business Survey. http://www.mzinga.com/

Susan Cain, *The Rise of the New Groupthink*, New York Times, Opinion Section, January 13, 2012

Wayne F. Cascio, *Managing Human Resources: Productivity, Quality of Work Life, Profits*, McGraw-Hill, 8th edition, 2009

Kevin P. Coyne and Shawn T. Coyne, *Brainsteering : A Better Approach to Breakthrough Ideas*, HarperCollins, 2011

Fast Company, http://www.fastcompany.com/most-innovative-companies/2011/

Karan Girotra, Christian Terwiesch, and Karl T. Ulrich, *Idea Generation and the Quality of the Best Idea*, Management Science, MS-01219-2007.R1, ScholarOne Manuscript Central, 2007

Kenji Hiranabe, "Visualizing Agile Projects using Kanban Boards," http://www.infoq.com/articles/agile-kanban-boards, accessed November, 2011

Larry Huston and Nabil Sakkab, *Connect and Develop: Inside Proctor & Gamble's New Model for Innovation*, Harvard Business Review, R0603C-PDF-ENG, March 2006

R. S. Kaplan and D. P. Norton, "The Balanced Scorecard – Measures that Drive Performance," Harvard Business Review, January 1992

Ron LeFleur, "The Responsibility Matrix (Circle Dot Chart)," http://www.ttoolboxes.ca/blog/index.cfm/2008/10/18/The-Responsibility-Matrix-Circle-Dot-Chart, accessed November 2011

Jeffrey Liker and Walton Hancock, *Organizational Systems Barriers to Engineering Effectiveness*, IEEE Transactions on Engineering Management, EM-33 (2), 1986, pp. 82-91

Merriam-Webster Dictionary, 10th Edition, Merriam-Webster, Incorporated, Springfield, MA. 1996

Merriam-Webster Dictionary, http://www.merriam-webster.com/ dictionary/execution, accessed January 2012

Andrew S. Rappaport and Shmuel Halevi, "The Computerless Computer Company," Harvard Business Review, 1991, http://hbr.org/1991/07/the-computerless-computer-company/ar/1, accessed September 2011

Eric Ries, *The Lean Startup*, Crown Business Press, 2011

David Robertson, *Platform Product Development*, Baan Company, March 1998

Arthur Schneiderman, "Setting Quality Goals," Quality Progress, April 1988

George Stalk Jr. and Thomas M. Hout, *Competing Against Time*, Free Press, 1990

Christian Terwiesch and Karl Ulrich, *Innovation Tournaments: Creating and Selecting Exceptional Opportunities*, Harvard Business School Press, May 2009

Warren Toomey, *The Strange Birth and Long Life of Unix*, IEEE Spectrum, December 2011, pp. 34-55

Steven Wheelwright and Kim Clark, *Revolutionizing Product Development: Quantum Leaps in Speed, Efficiency, and Quality*, Free Press, 2011

Nigel Wood, "Learning to See: How Does Your Supply Chain Function?" http://www.littoralis.info/iom/secure/assets/iom20041213.753113_41bde1a9d4ef.pdf, accessed October 2011

Index